The Amazing Money Machine

How to Make Money and Build a Passive Income Owning and Operating ATM Machines

By Noah C. Wieder

Publisher of ATMDepot.com

Free Gift

Thank you so much for purchasing my book!

As a thank you, and to get our relationship started right, I'd love to offer you a FREE GIFT. To get your gift, simply head on over to ATMDepot.com/gift.

Why You Should Read This Book.

Are you tired of how to make money books, passive income books, and get rich books that make it seem so easy? Most passive income books involve making money online, which requires you to learn how to sell stuff on Amazon, create ads on Facebook, become an online affiliate marketer, write a blog and sell ad space, build an ecommerce website, create a smartphone app, create an email list, write sales copy, or a host of other online businesses where you'd have to learn a lot about computers, the Internet, and how to hire virtual assistants to complete all of the necessary tasks.

You could also buy and rent real estate, trade stocks, join some MLM (and try to convince your friends that it's awesome), learn about flipping houses, or some other real estate venture. Wow, so many ways, it can make your head spin, right?

Well, fortunately, this book is none of those. This book is all about how to make money from a nice passive income by operating an ATM business. A simple machine (think of it like a vending machine, except the only inventory is $20 bills, no snacks, no soda, no spoilage) that you can purchase one time and have it pay for itself over and over, month after month, generating fantastic passive income without having to keep up with technology changes or convincing your family and friends to buy stuff from you.

I'll even let you in on some secrets that show you how to earn a passive income in the ATM business without even having to actually buy, own, or operate the Automated Teller Machines (ATMs) themselves.

I'm fairly certain if you're reading this that you've used an ATM before and have probably wondered why you have to pay a fee to get your own money. You may have also thought about who gets that fee and thought that it was the banks that did.

Well, if you use non-bank branded ATMs (typically the ones in retail stores, office buildings, bars, etc.), the owner of the ATM usually gets to keep that fee (or most of it) and, that fee, well, it adds up fast. **Wouldn't you like to collect that $2.50 (average fee) for every person who uses an ATM?**

Let's look at a quick example: Suppose only eight people per day use an ATM machine; that's $20 per day in fees collected. Those eight people per day can earn the ATM Owner $600 per month, and that's just from one machine. If you owned and operated that ATM, it's all yours. Suppose you operated an ATM, and it was a slow location. We're talking only four people per day used it; that's still $300 per month. So, how do people own and operate ATMs? You'll just have to finish reading this book to find out.

Once you become familiar with the terminology (which is pretty easy), this will be one of the easiest businesses you've ever seen. This is not a get rich quick book, and it will take some effort in the beginning. Running an ATM business does require work, as does anything that makes you money. And, if you really focus and are serious about learning this business, you will make a lot of money. Once you are earning a passive income at the level you want, you can either continue to grow, or you can simply kick back and count your money.

What this book can help you do is to learn the entire ATM business. It does not guarantee your success. You see, successful people put what they have learned into action and keep trying until they succeed. The action part is up to you.

Whether you are looking to switch from your routine 9 to 5, set up a full-fledged ATM business of your own, or simply supplement your income and make a few extra bucks on autopilot each month from a nice passive income, the idea of investing in ATMs is really fantastic. The capital outlay required is limited. It's one of the least expensive legitimate businesses you can start and make money from almost immediately.

You don't need to have any significant entrepreneurial experience, and again, you don't need to learn to sell stuff online, join an MLM, pay franchise fees, or flip houses. If you already do any of those, this business will be a breeze.

This is the perfect alternative for anyone looking to make a passive income in their spare time as well. There is great potential in running an ATM business properly, and that is what this book is all about.

This book will provide you with all of the information you need to operate your own ATM business successfully, as well as how to avoid the mistakes I made when I first started.

This book is not going to talk about how to set up business entities like an LLC, or if you should incorporate, or if you should be a sole proprietor. There are plenty of books about that topic already.

If you want to keep it simple, just start doing business as yourself. You don't need to set up a business to own or operate an ATM Machine when you first start off.

The key to success is to take imperfect action and get started. If you wait for everything to be perfect, you'll never get going.

Use this book as your guide. It will teach you everything about buying an ATM and making profits. From getting started with your business to learning to operate the machine, you will find tips and instructions on virtually everything you need to know about running a successful ATM business.

The only thing I ask in return is for you to **read this entire book all the way through to the very end**. Only then will you be able to make the most of the information provided.

Once you've finished reading this book, to get more in-depth information, including how-to videos, you can visit atmdepot.com.

Table of Contents

About The Author

Noah Wieder is a serial entrepreneur, speaker, publisher, and author. He has been in the ATM Business since 1993 and built two successful ATM businesses from the ground up. The first was XtraCash ATM, which started in 1996 and was subsequently sold in 2000 to CIBC (a large Canadian Bank). CIBC then sold the XtraCash division in 2002 to E*Trade.

Noah is currently the CEO of Intelligent eCommerce, Inc. which began as Wieder Marketing Int'l in 1994 and now operates ATMDepot.com. He is also the CEO of SearchBug, Inc (an online public records search firm).

Noah resides in San Diego, California with his family and can sometimes be found riding his bicycle to the office near Moonlight Beach.

Noah really enjoys teaching and has taught hundreds and hundreds of people how to operate a successful ATM business. He finally decided to put all of his ATM teachings into a book about the business to help as many people as possible.

If you are serious about earning a passive income and starting or growing an ATM Business, Noah sincerely hopes you read all of the way through this book, and that his experience can put much more money into your pocket, as well as help you avoid costly mistakes.

Throughout this book, Noah mentions resources he's made available at ATMDepot.com. Please, go there! This book, and the tools he provides to support you, offer the best of everything he's heard, seen, studied, and experienced. Please use them.

Disclaimer / Legal Notices / Copyright and Trademark Notices

allow the exclusion of implied warranties, so the above exclusion may not apply to you. Under no circumstances, including, but not limited to, negligence, shall the Author be liable for any special or consequential damages that result for the use of or the inability to use this book, even if the Author or his/her authorized representative has been advised of the possibility of such damages. In no event shall the Author's total liability to you for all damages, losses, and causes of actions (whether in contract, tort, including but not limited to, negligence or otherwise) exceed the amount paid by you, if any, for this book. Facts and information are believed to be accurate at the time they were placed in this book. All data provided in this book is to be used for informational purposes only. The information contained within is not intended to provide specific legal, financial, or tax advice, or any other advice whatsoever, for any individual or company and should not be relied upon in that regard. The services described are only offered in jurisdictions where they may be legally offered. Information provided is not all-inclusive and is limited to information that is made available, and such information should not be relied upon as all inclusive or accurate.

This book contains hyperlinks to websites and information created and maintained by the Author as well as other individuals and organizations. The Author does not control or guarantee the accuracy, completeness, relevance, or timeliness of any information or privacy policies posted on these linked websites. You should assume that all references to products and services in this book are made because material connections exist between the Author and the providers of the mentioned products and/or services ("Providers"). You should also assume that all hyperlinks within this book are affiliate links for either (a) the Author or (b) someone else who is an affiliate for the mentioned product or service (individually and collectively, the "Affiliate"). The Affiliate recommends products and services in this book based in part on a good faith belief that the purchase of such products or services will help readers in general.

No Earnings Projections, Promises or Representations for purposes of this disclaimer. Any earnings or income statements, or earnings or income examples, are only estimates of what the Author thinks you could earn. There is no assurance you'll do as well. If you rely upon the Author's figures, you must accept the risk of not doing as well. Where specific income figures are used and attributed to an individual or business, those persons or businesses have earned that amount. There is no assurance you'll do as well. If you rely upon our figures, you must accept the risk of not doing as well. Any and all claims or representations as to income earnings in this book are not to be considered as average earnings. There can be no assurance that any prior successes or past results as to income earnings can be used as an indication of your future success or results. Monetary and income results are based on many factors. We have no way of knowing how well you will do, as we do not know you, your background, your work ethic, or your business skills or practices. Therefore, we do not guarantee or imply that you will generate any passive income, that you will do as well, or you will make any money at all. There is no assurance you'll do as well. If you rely upon our figures, you must accept the risk of not doing as well. ATM businesses and earnings derived therefrom have unknown risks involved and are not suitable for everyone. Making decisions based on any information presented in this book should be done only with the knowledge that you could experience a loss or make no money at all. The information presented in this book is for educational and informational purposes only. Use caution and seek the advice of qualified professionals. Check with your accountant, lawyer or professional advisor before acting on this or any information. The information in this book should be carefully considered and evaluated before reaching a business decision on whether to rely on them or not. You agree that the Author is not responsible for the success or failure of your business decisions relating to any information presented herein. In no event shall the Author be liable for any direct, indirect, incidental, punitive, or consequential damages of any kind whatsoever with respect to the service, the materials and the products contained within. This book is not intended to be a substitute to professional advice.

Materials in this book may contain information that includes or is based upon forward-looking statements within the meaning of the Securities Litigation Reform Act of 1995. Forward-looking statements give the Author's expectations for forecasts of future events. You can identify these statements by the fact that they do not relate strictly to historical or current facts. They use words such as "anticipate," "believe," "estimate," "expect," "intend," "plan," "project," and other words and terms of similar meaning in connection with a description of potential earnings or financial performance. Any and all forward-looking statements here or on any materials in this book are intended to express an opinion of earnings potential. Many factors will be important in determining your actual results. And no guarantees are made that you will achieve similar results to the Author or anyone else; in fact, no guarantees are made that you will achieve any results from the Author's ideas and techniques found in this book.

Author's History

I graduated from college in 1984 in Upstate New York with a Bachelor's of Science in Business and a minor in Computer sciences. I had no idea what to do with that degree, but I knew I didn't want to stay in New York. So, in the summer of 1984, I packed up everything I owned in a 1978 Chevy Van and headed west to San Diego. (That two-week trip could be my next book.)

I'd had enough of the snow and cold and was ready to start my career (even though I had no idea what that was going to be).

Upon reaching San Diego at just 21 years old, I had no job and not much savings, so I needed to figure out what to do quickly. I perused the local newspaper classified section (there were no internet or job boards in the early 80's) and answered a few classified ads. I quickly landed a commission-only job selling stuff door to door (if you had a pulse, they hired you). After several successful months selling stuff door to door, I figured that if I could be successful in door-to-door sales, working in a car dealership selling cars to people actually interested in cars should be much better than selling stuff nobody really needed. I went back to the classified section once again and discovered that a lot of car dealers were advertising for sales people.

It was odd; almost every car dealer I interviewed with offered me a job. I was young, and the Jeep dealer and the Toyota dealer were offering the best commissions at the time. Still no salaried positions, but getting paid for production was fine with me. I was hungry and willing to talk to people, no problem. So, I took a sales position with Toyota selling used cars (yep, I was officially a used car salesman). I sold new cars also, but I could only take an "up" on the used car lot. An "up" refers to the prospective buyer and is a generic term for any potential customer who walks onto a car lot. Sales people take turns talking to those customers.

I actually really enjoyed talking to people about their cars and even their current car problems. Without knowing it at the time, I was actually offering them a solution to their existing car woes. That's why selling cars seemed pretty easy and enjoyable for a while. I did very well my first year, actually being honored as car salesman back in the day.

Since I didn't envision myself as a car salesman forever, and while it was good money for being in my 20's, it was not that fulfilling. Plus, it got very competitive with the career salesmen. I think management may have hired young, hungry sales people to keep the seasoned career car salesmen from getting lazy.

In my pursuit of a job where I could use my business degree and potentially find a real career, I continued my job search. With the help of some networking, I eventually landed at The Price Company (now Costco).

I worked at the Price Company (aka Price Club) for almost 4 years, starting at the bottom in the accounting department. I felt like I had something to prove, and since I was only making minimum wage in a union shop, I had to climb my way up the ladder. I eventually went on to become an accounting supervisor, then a staff accountant, and that eventually led me to the buying office where I managed office supplies and electronic SKUs for dozens of warehouses.

While working at the Price Club was a great job and thought it could be a career, I really envisioned having my own company someday. Not having to answer to a boss, sleeping in late when I wanted, and working towards a goal of financial freedom. After all, it is the American Dream.

I always wanted to have my own business, and with the help of a college friend, we set out to do that in 1989 as one of the first Snapple Distributors outside of New York. Owning your own business has its benefits, but it also means you have to do whatever it takes to get the job done. Suffice it to say, I did not get to sleep in. It was many long nights, 7 days a week, and barely 1 year later, the debt mounted and we ran out of money. I eventually sold the distributorship at a loss.

That was my first of many failed attempts at entrepreneurship. Each failure added to my entrepreneurial experience, which could fill several other books. Suffice it to say that after many other failed business attempts and a job in the merchant processing business, I started in the ATM business in 1993. I was working for a check guarantee company when the partners formed a company called U.S. ATM.

U.S. ATM was the first distributor for a new type of ATM called a "script machine." Script machines were small countertop machines that accepted ATM cards but dispensed a voucher good for cash. You took this voucher to the cash register of the retail location or bar tender if in a bar (where the script machines were popular) to pay for your goods and get the balance back in cash.

Within a few months, U.S. ATM became one of the first distributors for Tidel ATM machines. Within a few months after that, I became a certified technician for Tidel ATMs.

Back then, salesmen would go door to door in San Diego and Las Vegas selling Tidel AnyCard ATM (aka Tidel Tube Machine, pictured right).

In 1994, I was approached by the CEO of National Bankcard Association, Inc. (NBA) to run their Merchant Processing sales division. Upon successfully re-launching their merchant sales division, a year later, in 1995, I founded XtraCash ATM as a subsidiary of NBA.

NBA started to grow quickly, which eventually led to an investment by venture capitalist firm JMI, John Moores Investments (John served on the NBA board until it was sold in 2001). We quickly grew from just 14 employees to over 100 within a few years.

XtraCash ATM became one of the top 5 ATM companies in the country at that time, managing close to 5,000 ATMs in just 5 years.

During the mid to late 90s, I was fortunate to be one of a select few individuals appointed to the first ever Triton Advisory committee and served two years in that capacity. Triton is still a leader in ATM machine manufacturing today, and is the only freestanding ATM made in the USA.

As part of the XtraCash growth strategy, I trained hundreds if not thousands of individuals, conducted dozens of sales training and coaching seminars for ATM distributors, and successfully negotiated contracts representing thousands of locations, including 170+ Southern California McDonald's locations. I'm not trying to brag; I'm simply trying to relate that my experience most certainly validates the information I've presented to you on the pages in this book.

In 2000, XtraCash ATM was sold to Canadian Imperial Bank of Commerce, (CIBC) a very large Canadian Bank. They wanted to use our network of ATMs as access points for their newly launched Internet Bank called Amicus.

In 2001, my article "Are ATMs the New Plastic," was featured in Transaction World which you can view by typing this short link into your computer browser.

http://bit.ly/1AFVmpB

In 2002, CIBC's plans changed, and they closed Amicus and sold off the ATM division to E*Trade. I was invited to join the E*Trade team in Arlington, VA; however, my preference was to stay in San Diego.

That's when I spent the next year taking everything I learned over the previous decade and put that experience to work developing a new and better way to help others become Independent ATM Deployers.

In 2003, I launched ATMDepot.com which currently helps hundreds of IADs successfully operate ATMs nationwide.

As of this writing, our family of IADs operates well over a thousand machines, and our ATM network dispenses millions and millions of dollars in ATM cash monthly to customers.

This book compiles the last 20+ years of my experience in the ATM Business in hopes that it can help you to build wealth and a healthy passive income by deploying ATM machines in your city.

It doesn't take thousands or even hundreds of machines to build a nice residual income. You can start your passive income now with as little as one machine, or you can even start making a passive income in the ATM business without even owning any ATMs, but you'll have to finish the book to find out about all of these options.

Introduction

Did you know that there are close to half a million automated teller machines (ATMs) currently in operation in the US (as of 2015)? While the number continues to grow, as the convenience of being able to withdraw cash without having to go to the bank has attracted many people over the years, there is still plenty of opportunity.

What may come as no surprise is that most ATMs aren't owned by financial institutions (banks and credit unions). More than half of the ATMs in operation in the USA today are owned and operated by independent ATM Deployers (IADs) or Independent Sales Organizations (ISOs).

While ISOs are typically larger organizations that pay large fees to be registered with the networks, IADs can be anyone, from a single person (like you) to a group of individuals. IADs typically invest their money in an ATM and generate income through it, or they help Merchants and Retailers manage their own ATMs and share in the profits. ISOs typically concentrate on the latter.

Given the fact that there is more paper currency in circulation in the world today than ever before, the demand for ATMs is unlikely to go down anytime soon; thus, setting up your own ATM business is still very lucrative.

Getting Started

Before moving on to the business side of things, it is important to familiarize yourself with the concepts and terminology of running an ATM business. On the surface, it may sound as though you have to sell ATMs. However, this isn't necessarily the case at all. While you can do that if you like, the most lucrative and highest passive income opportunity is when you purchase an ATM and install it at a good location. You become the Bank, the ATM Owner and Operator.

You make money every time your ATM is used. This isn't a 'get rich quick' method, so you shouldn't consider it as one. This is a legitimate business opportunity where you can make a decent return on your investment. It does require you to work at it (a few hours a week) to be successful.

Many IADs earn an annualized return of 35% - 70% or more. With Banks paying hardly any interest these days, there isn't much opportunity for safe investments. The stock market fluctuates, bonds and mutual funds go up and down, and there are numerous ways real estate investing can be risky.

More and more smart investors are turning to owning their own ATM Machines. It's quite simple really. The beautiful thing about this business is how fast you start making money without having to invest too much money in the first place. There is one caveat: the longer you wait to start your ATM business, the longer it takes to build your passive income, and the more competition you could face in your area.

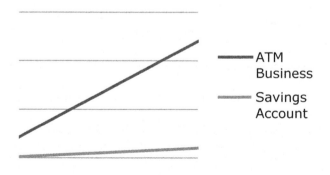

So let's take a look at some basics of how an ATM business works.

How Does the ATM Business Work?

There is a surprising lack of awareness about the ATM business. The general perception is that ATMs are operated by banks and other financial institutions, so most people don't even bother inquiring about them. Most ATM businesses are actually run independently. Though more IADs are stepping into the arena, there are still no major barriers to entry.

So, the time is ripe for you to consider having your own ATM business. However, before that, you need to know how the business works. There are four steps involved in setting up an ATM business:

Step 1: Choosing a Location

Like every successful business does, you have to spot a gap in the market. Every entrepreneur is able to see potential. I'm sure you will be able to find locations near where you live, work, or play that can use an ATM. It could be a retail store, restaurant, nightclub, adult store, shopping arcade, a commercial building, manufacturing facility, festival, event, or any place where people go. The key is to determine whether or not there is enough foot traffic there to make it a profitable venture.

 The other opportunity is to find locations around you that already have ATMs but where the equipment may be old, outdated, non-compliant, out of order often, or owned and operated by someone who is no longer keeping it maintained, possibly due to life-changing circumstances like health or family issues.

The 'gap,' therefore, becomes the location where you think an ATM is needed, where the location wants a newer ATM, where the ownership has changed, or where whoever is in charge wants to work with a different person for various reasons.

Step 2: Buy or Lease an ATM

The next step is buying or leasing an ATM. There are many ATM Companies that sell these machines, so it shouldn't be too difficult for you to find and select one. A simple online search is all it takes for you to get into touch with a reputable ATM company. You can place an order for the machine, which will then be delivered to you at a specified place at an agreed-upon date and time. Once you have the machine in hand, the fun begins.

Step 3: Programming & Installing the Machine

The ATM has to be programmed (or re-programmed if you buy a used model or take over the management of a previously installed one) for processing. Without ATM processing, people won't be able to withdraw money from the ATM. In other words, it would be worthless. If you're far from tech-savvy, you will want to hire a professional to program the machine for you. When you contact an ATM company that offers ATM processing, you will complete the required paperwork to get your machine set up in their system. Then you or a technician will obtain programming instructions. That is when you will get your machine's Terminal ID (TID) number that is unique to it alone. Installation can be done by the ATM company's installer, or you can decide to unbox the ATM and bolt it to the floor yourself.

Step 4: Load the Cash

The last step is loading the machine with cash. You need to have sufficient funds (cash) in the ATM for people to be able to withdraw the amount they need. Up until 2012, the average withdrawal transaction was $60; now, it's a little more. That aside, you'll need to know the capacity of the ATM you have purchased in terms of the amount of money it can hold. Most Deployer's purchase ATMs come standard with a 700 or 1,700 note cassette. Unless you have a really busy location, you would rarely need to fill the ATM to capacity. We'll discuss cash needs more in depth later, but the reality is that you can start with as little as 100 or so $20 bills and then use online reports and text alerts to tell you when you need to add more cash.

These steps illustrate how the ATM business works. You buy the machine and set it up at a location of your choice. The machine is then made available to the public, and they can use it to withdraw cash from their checking, savings, or other accounts associated with the ATM card used. You will receive a fee (which you decide upon) for each cash withdrawal transaction made on your ATM. This is your revenue from the business. It is only a matter of time before your revenue increases to a point that your original investment is recouped and you start making a big profit.

Keep in mind that this is a basic premise of how the ATM business works. There is a little more to this than simply buying a machine and installing it. You will have to complete the required banking paperwork, provide proper documentation and pass a basic background check. As long as you have not committed a felony or financial crime, you would most likely pass. While the ATM business is pretty simple, there are issues that may arise from time to time as with any business.

Don't let this discourage you. Running an ATM business may sound complex, but in reality, it is quite easy. There is little business-like activity involved, and you don't have to make many tough decisions. However, if you have your doubts, reading this book until the end will quell them for sure. All of the information you need about an ATM business is provided here. So, you shouldn't run into any unknown issues or face too many hassles once your business is up and running.

How Do You Make Money In The ATM Business?

Now that you know a little bit about how the ATM business works, it is time to discuss how you make money. Keep in mind that while the business is highly lucrative, and you can build wealth, you need to keep it professional. Do things the right way and don't create shortcuts. Don't treat your business like a hobby. It's a real business. Wherever you place your ATMs, those business people will be counting on you. **It's your reputation and networking skills that will help to grow your business.** Technically, there are two ways in which you can make money from an ATM:

1. ATM Surcharge

If you choose (which more ATM owners do), you would levy a fee on the transactions people perform on the ATM you own; this is called the Surcharge. For instance, if a person withdraws $100 from his/her checking or savings account using your ATM, a fee would be charged, usually $2.50 (but we suggest you adhere to what other ATMs in the area are charging; more on this later). You earn this surcharge since you are providing a service in the sense that you are saving people a trip to their bank to get cash. There are some ways you can increase the surcharge and usage, which we will discuss in a later chapter. If you work with ATMDepot.com, you keep the entire surcharge. I will discuss more on this later as well.

2. ATM Interchange

You can also get a share of the fee charged by the network your ATM is connected to. The fee, known as interchange, is imposed by ATM networks on the banks to interconnect their bank with other ATMs. In this case, you may receive a few additional cents on cash transactions from the ATM company you deal with. This also depends on the ATM network (which is determined based on the cardholders ATM card), thus, increasing your earnings considerably over time.

Some ATM companies don't share any of the Interchange with their clients, while some ATM companies believe in transparency and work more like a partnership. If the ATM company you select shares some of the interchange, they will probably pass on the acquirer fees as well. In most cases, the Acquirer fees charged are typically less than the share of interchange, but this is also dependent on the type of ATM cards used at your location. You can always discuss the best strategy with your ATM processing provider.

A true partner will want you to be able to maximize your revenue while at the same time making money for everyone. Keep in mind that you want to make sure your ATM provider is making money so they answer the phones when you need help. If a deal seems too good to be true, it probably is. This is where an experienced ATM processing or service provider is critical.

These two ways of making money through an ATM business aren't mutually exclusive. They exist at the same time, enabling you to earn more than the basic surcharge or helping to offset some of the network fees imposed on ATM Transactions. Some networks, particularly the national networks (Plus & Cirrus) have what's called a tiered interchange structure as well as an acquirer fee. So, depending on the actual type of card used, the interchange and acquirer fees vary. International transactions cannot be surcharged and impose a completely different set of fees (this rarely affects regular ATMs unless you happen to have one in a very tourist-driven area). Some of the ATM processing companies pass all network-related costs through to the ATM owner or whoever is collecting the lion's share of the surcharge.

These fees are typically minimal compared to the surcharge collected and range from $0.01 to $0.18 and vary by network (ATM card used). Since ATM Owners don't typically bear any backend communication costs, bank sponsorship costs, or any of the other operational costs to complete ATM transactions, the fees generated from the use of the ATM are pure profit which, even after some minimal processing fees, deliver a great return on investment (ROI).

So, how much money can you expect to make in a month through your ATM business? As mentioned previously, the typical surcharge you earn per transaction is $2.50, and some ATM companies will pay you extra (the interchange to help offset any network or acquirer fees), but let's just use the surcharge to keep it simple. To calculate your monthly earnings, you simply need to multiply your surcharge amount by the number of transactions you expect to be performed on your ATM.

One Hundred and Eighty (180) is a very reasonable figure to use when it comes to estimating the number of transactions that are performed on an average non-bank ATM. This means that just 6 people have to perform a cash withdrawal transaction, on average, every day. That being said, there are several factors that determine the number of transactions performed. For instance, if your ATM is located in a place where the foot traffic is heavy and people spend a lot of cash, it is possible that you may get over 20 transactions performed on a daily basis.

Coming back to the point, if 180 transactions are performed on your ATM in a given month and your surcharge was $2.50, your monthly gross revenue from just one ATM would be approximately $450.

This is a great way to earn a passive income without doing much. Your ATM company should provide you with the support you need to keep your ATM up and running. However, if you are seriously considering building wealth with your ATM business, you have to increase the number of machines you have.

Having one machine to rely on for revenue is not going to do the trick. The more machines you have, the more money you will make. Also, it is important that you choose the location wisely. Of course, having more machines means more work, but the higher earnings and profits will justify the effort you have to put in.

There is good money to be made in an ATM business. You just need to know how to run it. You can use this option to generate extra income to supplement the wages from your day job, or when you're ready; you can tackle more locations and make this a full-time income. Once you've learned the business, are comfortable with the operation, and have placed 6 to 12 ATM machines in your local area, we suggest you set up a proper business if you have not done so already. Operating close to a dozen ATM machines will most likely mean your passive income will be dramatically more than your day job or most retirement investments.

It's very easy to manage a small network of a dozen or so ATM machines. Once the ATMs are in place, all that's left to do is to count the money, load the machines, and get paid.

As an example, if you had 12 machines averaging 180 transactions per month at a $2.50 surcharge you **would be making over $5,000 monthly**, and you could, most likely, **work less than 4 hours a week**. Regardless of how many ATMs you want to operate, you will be making money while you are sleeping.

Ownership & Responsibilities

Owning an ATM machine brings with it a set of responsibilities. You will be responsible for ensuring that the machine remains up and running throughout the day and that there is minimal, if any, downtime. Also, you need to take care of the legalities associated with running an ATM business, as well as bearing the costs of keeping the ATM operational.

This means that there are several things to take care of. As the owner, you have to be in charge. It is better to keep things under control and ensure everything goes smoothly. Of course, you have the option to delegate the responsibilities to people you trust, but then again, it is akin to ceding control. Yet, this may not necessarily be the case.

Before moving on to deciding the most important responsibility for running an ATM business, let's determine who owns the ATM.

Who Owns the ATM?

You might be confused to read the title of this topic. After all, since you ordered the ATM, you own it. There is no doubt that the person who orders the ATM, pays for it, and has it installed is the one who owns it. But, at the same time, you have to consider the fact that the location you are installing the machine in might be owned by someone else.

If you found an empty storefront, retail space, kiosk or other type of space and rented it, then you continue to retain ownership of the machine. However, in situations where you are using the space in someone else's store or business place, you will most likely have to split some revenue with them. In that case, it becomes a partnership rather than sole ownership. So, does the other party own the ATM?

The short answer is "No." The agreement between the parties that is drawn up is referred to as a site location agreement (SLA). An SLA will clearly state the name of the business where you are installing the ATM as the location and your name as the owner. Of course, the terms and conditions you decide with the other party may vary, but that doesn't mean you have to cede ownership. So, even if you have to share revenue with the location, you remain the owner of the ATM and reap the benefits of the fixed asset and its depreciation for tax purposes.

Who Loads the ATM?

Well, this is the million dollar question (or the thousand dollar one at least). The person who loads the ATM is known as the ATM Vaulter. The biggest responsibility you need to bear when operating an ATM business is to determine who is loading the ATM. Most ATM business owners load their own machines, at least until they get bigger. Loading the cash from time to time is really not as big a deal as it sounds.

It will take a while for you to determine how often to load it and how much cash each machine will need to be efficient with load times and vault cash. You can project the number of transactions you expect on the machine from the outset, but whether that number is accurate can only be discovered later on.

On average, an on-site ATM machine owner may load 40 to 50 $20 bills into the ATM machine on a daily or every other day basis. However, you would most likely be an off-site owner, since you will probably not be at the location every day. You will probably want to put in enough cash so that the ATM will not run out for at least a week. You don't want to be running to load the ATM every other day. It is quite possible that the number of transactions on your machine will exceed your expectations and, as such, you'll need to put in a hundred or so 20's (that would be a good thing).

While most ATMs will come standard with a cassette that will hold more than enough cash, you should become familiar with the different types. The types of cassettes and the number of notes they can hold are discussed in more detail in a later chapter.

Regardless of the number of transactions, it is a good idea to check up on your machine at least once a day or every other day even if you don't need to load it. This can be done remotely via the Internet if you're working with ATM Depot or another ATM provider that offers online real-time usage access.

If you are on-site, meaning you work in the store or very close by, and you don't have much cash to load, it is possible that you might need to load the machine daily. This is why it is important to determine who will load the machine. In most cases, the owner chooses to do this on his/her own.

However, you can also get someone to do the job for you. Make sure the person you select for the job is trustworthy and knows how to operate the machine and load the cassette (and is trained properly). If you don't feel you have someone worthy of delegating the job to, it is better to do it yourself or to talk to your ATM company and ask if they offer cash vaulting.

If you're managing your own vaulting, at least you can rest assured that the machine is always full of cash and there is no risk of you being swindled. Keep in mind that if you're loading the cash, it is most likely your cash going into the machine.

When installing a machine in someone else's store, you can also ask the store owner to be the vaulter as part of the arrangement if you so choose. Even though the store owner will only be the location and not the owner, this does not mean that he/she cannot be responsible for loading the ATM.

There are pros and cons to having the store be the vaulter. Pros include one less responsibility for you as the owner. You also can use your cash to purchase more equipment. The pro for the store owner is that it ensures him/her that the machine won't run out of cash; however, our experience tells us that if he/she forgets to load the cash, or is not always available, your machine will end up running out of cash anyway, and that is a con for you. You would also expect to pay the store owner more of the revenue if he/she is using his/her cash to load the ATM.

For your first few machines, we would suggest you load cash to experience the entire business process. If you are unable to load cash, your ATM provider may be able to provide you with a vaulter, but expect to pay either a flat fee or a flat per transaction charge. It's best to locate your first few machines within a 10 – 20 mile radius of your home or office so you can service them properly and get to know the business. Once you're experienced, you'll see many other natural opportunities.

The bottom line is that it isn't necessary that the same person own and load the ATM. It is a responsibility that can be given to someone else. You have to decide what's convenient for you in the long run. If you plan to set up a dozen ATMs all over town or in your nearby city, you may need some assistance getting the machines loaded.

The ownership and responsibilities related to the ATM machine will be decided upon before the site location agreement is drawn up.

More shall be revealed later on about cash loading, where to get cash, how to manage cash flow, and what to do if you run short on cash. We will also go over the contents of a site location agreement in more detail in a coming chapter

Location

Where to Find Locations?

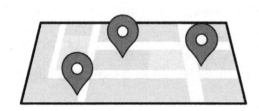

Location is perhaps the most important of all factors when it comes to an ATM business. Selecting the right location to install a machine more or less guarantees success. Yet, there are many people who select the wrong locations.

Select a poor location for your ATM, you end up making a lot less than you should, and your ROI takes too long. However, even a poor location (we consider 2 transactions daily or less to be poor) can still turn an annualized return of 25% - 30%.

It's hard to lose money in the ATM business, but it can still happen if you choose a really bad location. The nice thing is that you can always move the ATM to a new or better location. The ATM business can be very lucrative, but only if you work the business and do the right things. Finding, selecting, and obtaining good locations should be at the top of your agenda.

There are various factors that determine whether or not a location is perfect for installing an ATM or not. Let's look at some of them:

Proximity to Nearest ATM

Where can you expect a large number of people to come in and use your machine? Of course, at a location where there isn't an ATM nearby. So, the first thing you have to keep in mind is the proximity of your machine to the nearest ATM location.

Commercial avenues usually have a number of ATM machines on the same street. Installing a machine there only makes sense if one or more of these factors exist: If your surcharge is lower; if foot traffic is high; or if other ATMs are old or outdated.

Proximity to Retail Outlets

People need cash when they go shopping. It is convenient for them to withdraw the cash where they are shopping and doing daily errands. If your ATM can help people to save time and is more convenient than an ATM somewhere else, your ATM will be preferred. This is why setting up an ATM close to retail outlets, busy coffee shops, bars, quick service or casual restaurants, and many other establishments is a good idea. Many of these locations have ATMs, but there are always opportunities. Many of the ATMs in these places may be old or outdated models in need of an upgrade or the service providers have disappeared. Look for out-o- order ATMs or machines that appear to be in need of some TLC. If you see an opportunity, inquire with the manager or store personnel to find out if there is a problem that you can help solve. Everyone loves and wants the newest, best machine.

Proximity to Your Residence/Workplace

If your ATM business model requires that you will be loading the cash into your ATMs or the locations you secure want you to be full service and load the cash, it can sometimes be difficult if you live too far from your ATM machines. Consider the traffic, mileage and other costs when determining locations. Though this might impact your business to some extent, it is best to find a location that is close to your home or office to start with. Once you fully understand the business, you can spread out, but we find there are plenty of opportunities closer than most think. If you start with a very nearby location, you can easily check the machine from time to time until your comfort level increases. This is the one way you can ensure your ATM business gets off the ground running smoothly.

Apart from these three considerations, you also need to keep in mind the rent you may have to pay if you don't own the space in which the machine is to be installed. We will provide you a number of options as to the best locations for installing an ATM in the next part of this chapter.

What Are Some of the Best ATM Locations?

It is hard to come up with reliable estimates for the number of transactions performed at a particular ATM location. There are differences in terms of region and season. For instance, an ATM located in a casino usually attracts more transactions on average than ATMs in other locations. Yet, there can be some ATMs installed in casinos that don't get that many transactions.

According to our experience, the average number of transactions you can expect on your ATM is 150 to 180 a month. That is roughly 5 to 6 transactions per day. Yet, there are some locations that have reported a much higher average than this. Here are some of the best ATM locations you should consider installing a machine at if you have a way in to these types of venues. These venues often already have ATM machines, so it may take knowing someone in order to replace the current vendor.

Large Casinos – 1,500 to 3,000 transactions (sometimes more) monthly

Large Casinos are difficult to obtain and are often controlled by banks, but it is not unusual to try and get these types of accounts depending on who you know or what you can offer. If you already work with these types of accounts offering other services, adding the ATM to your arsenal of products is a much easier way in.

Smaller Casinos – 300 to 800 transactions monthly

Gentlemen's Clubs – 300 to 800 transactions monthly

While Gentlemen's clubs are very profitable ATM locations, they are also coveted locations and, hence, have higher competition. If you know someone at these locations or already have a relationship with these locations, it's an easier way in.

Without an "in," we would not suggest you start your ATM business by approaching the aforementioned location areas. Wet your feet with more easily obtainable locations and gain experience in the business, then go after more difficult locations. Later on in this book, I will reveal where you can get my private collection of ATM sales scripts that can help you to get started. Generally, these scripts are for cold calling; however, we do not recommend cold calling store owners with this opportunity. The scripts I'll reveal later are to help you find out who the owner is so you can send him/her an email or visit him/her in person and check out the business. After all, you're investing in a machine that can help him/her increase his/her business. You are not selling him/her anything.

The surcharge is usually higher at the three aforementioned locations, making them highly lucrative for you. The following locations are more typical and often more easily obtainable.

Hotels (number of transactions depends on occupancy)
>   Small – 100 to 150 transactions monthly (Hotel or Motel with less than 150 rooms)
>   Medium – 100 to 200 transactions (Non-branded Hotels)
>   Large well-known brands – Over 200 transactions

Nightclubs & Bars – 250 to 500 transactions

Convenience Stores & Gas Stations – 200 to 400 transactions

Restaurants
>   Fast Food – 75 to 150 transactions
>   Quick Service – 100 to 150 transactions
>   Diners, Cafes & Luncheonettes – 150 to 200 transactions

Barbers & Nail/Hair Salons

Believe it or not, we have many of these locations doing quite well. Some of them average 8 - 10 transactions daily, resulting in 250 – 300 monthly transactions. These are locations where stylists often rent chairs or where there are several dozen manicurists, and the management doesn't accept credit cards due to the high fees. Also, customers like to tip in cash and often will just pay with cash if an ATM is nearby. If the surcharge is reasonable ($2.00), you can do quite well with larger nail salons or a salon building where there are many independent salon owners under one roof.

Microbreweries & Parking Lots

There are new locations popping up everywhere you look. Think of the places you visit often or the new places opening soon that you see locally. If they seem to have a lot of patrons, but don't have an ATM, that's an opportunity for you. If you go there often, so do other folks.

All transaction numbers indicated above are based on a calendar month. Based on our experience, installing an ATM at these locations yields, on average, the number of transactions mentioned, but your experience may vary, and there are no guarantees any location mentioned will meet the numbers provided. These are based solely on my experience over the last several decades I've been in the ATM business.

As you can see, the top locations are the ones where people are more likely to spend large amounts of cash. The only issue is that most of these locations already have an ATM on hand. Therefore, you might not find many empty spaces. However, a new machine is preferred over old ones. Plus, you can customize your ATM with special graphic packages to match the surroundings, which will surely attract customers.

While these are the best locations in terms of profitability and revenue, you can still make a decent annualized return from any location that offers you 80 - 100 transactions a month. At that rate, you will be able to enjoy a 40% to 70% return on investment annually. So, keep these locations in mind when you are trying to find spots to install your ATMs.

Check local trend and entertainment rags and subscribe to new business lists from your local or county service.

What If I Own a Retail Store?

If you own a retail store, adding an ATM machine is easy and could be the most profitable floor space in the store. The small footprint of the ATM takes up just over 1 square foot, or you can install a thru-the-wall machine to face the outside. This will help attract even more customers, which can increase the revenues of your business considerably. An ATM business can be highly lucrative and can bolster the revenue of your existing retail store.

Since the ATM machine is a new addition to your business, it is important that it is visible and well-advertised with signage so people use it, even if they weren't planning to go into your store.

If you want to draw a lot of attention to start things off, you can offer incentives for customers to use your machine to entice withdrawals. For instance, one of the fastest ways to build your ATM usage is to start with a very low surcharge and advertise it. If you charge less than most of the competition in the area, this will definitely get people to consider using your ATM.

If you do consider starting with a low surcharge, you'll need to consider how long this will remain. Increasing or changing your surcharge amount may require the ATM to have new master keys (programming) performed. Most ATM owners can do this themselves; however, some prefer to have a technician complete the task, so there may be a fee associated with a technician visit if required. Check with your ATM company before determining your surcharge amount if using it as an incentive.

There are many other ways to incentivize customers to use your ATM. Incentives can include all sorts of coupons printed on the receipt or printed separately, depending on the type of equipment. Talk to your ATM sales representative about ideas and options to help you to determine the best way to fully monetize your ATM.

Since most of the newer model ATMs have large graphic screens, it is important to work with a company that will help you to take advantage of the screen of the ATM. Be sure the ATM company you work with offers custom screen graphics so you can load your logo or other images onto your ATM to display eye-catching graphics.

Optimizing the ATM display will capture the attention of the people heading into your store so that they make a withdrawal there and then. While it is incredibly convenient for them to be able to withdraw cash from the machine when walking into the store, it is important for you as a store owner that they pay with cash instead of using their credit cards.

So, if you own a retail store, investing in an ATM can give your business a big boost. It not only offers convenience to your customers, it can lower your credit card fees by offering your customers cash, earn you big profits from surcharge fees, and offers customers coupons that build loyalty. While we just scratched the surface, there are many other benefits to owning and operating an ATM if you own a retail store.

What If I Own or Know Someone With a Commercial Building?

A commercial building is also a good location for an ATM, especially if it has a cafeteria or a large company that rents the space. It might be likely that other machines have already been installed there, so it's best to inquire. If this isn't the case, you should not hesitate to get one installed.

Shopping malls, small strip centers, and parking lots can also be wonderful locations. Look for small busy shopping centers where they might be too small for a bank to deploy an ATM.

These are often good locations, and the easiest way to find out who to speak with is to find out who handles the leasing for the tenants. Almost any tenant would give you the leasing manager's contact information, since it's not unlikely as merchants they'll think about getting some kind of referral fee or gratitude of appreciation from the leasing manager, especially when it's time to renew their own lease.

Can I install an ATM where I work?

You definitely can. However, keep in mind that if people know you own the ATM, they may get jealous that you are making all of the money from the fee. All kidding aside, you want to make sure there are enough people interested and you don't hide the ATM in the break room.

The key here is that there needs to be hundreds of employees. If the company where you work only has 50 or 100 employees and no cafeteria or a place to spend money, it's difficult to charge your coworkers $2.50 for cash if it's not that convenient for them to spend the cash they get. Sure, on paydays, you may get a bunch of transactions, but if that's only two times a month, you aren't going to make a killing. Granted, you can always move the ATM somewhere else, but I'd suggest speaking to us or an experienced service provider to help you navigate this type of deal.

Can I Put An ATM in a Condo Complex? What Should I Expect?

Yes, you can install an ATM in a condo complex. There are no restrictions on where you can install an ATM machine. However, you will need to get HOA approval if this is required. In many locations, this may not be ideal. The reason is plain and simple: the number of customers. If you install an ATM in a complex with only a few condos, you cannot expect too much business. If you can realistically expect at least 3 – 4 transactions a day in any location, this would be the bare minimum to have a decent return on investment. With the cost of equipment these days, it's getting easier to find profitable locations.

As always, if you're just starting out, discuss any potential locations with the ATM company or processing provider you choose. Be sure you speak with someone who has been in the business a long time and personally operates ATMs on a daily basis, not some desk jockey or quarterback salesman.

Revenue Split - If ATM is installed in Someone's Store

If you are operating the ATM as a business and enter into an agreement with a store owner to place your ATM in his/her location, it's very similar to the vending machine business.

Setting up an ATM in someone else's store often requires that you compensate him/her for use of the space. We'll use the term 'rent,' but often enough, it's more like a revenue share or revenue split deal. Whatever compensation or rent you agree on will be the monthly expense for the location. You'll have to calculate that into your projected revenues and expenses.

It is a given that you have to pay the store owner something for the space the ATM occupies. However, in the case of installing an ATM in the store, the location owner will also benefit. According to statistics, around 30% of the cash withdrawn from ATMs located in stores is spent in that store. This means that the store's sales should get a boost from the ATM being installed there. Moreover, we often see that if the location accepts credit cards, their credit card acceptance will be offset by ATM usages, thus lowering their credit card processing fees. We've even seen some locations completely abandon credit card acceptance once the ATM was installed.

Moreover, since you are operating an ATM business, it's best to collaborate with the store owner to ensure it's a win-win for you both. After all, if your business is new, it could take some time to establish a few good clients for a referral list. Setting up your machine in a well-known store will not only give your business credibility, but will give you exposure and earn you and the store owner profits.

The best way to strike a deal with the store owner is to share the revenue. This way, it becomes a partnership or co-op of sorts, and you can also split responsibilities with the store owner. While there are just a few things that need to be taken care of when operating an ATM machine, someone needs to do them. The tasks include loading cash (the Vaulter), loading receipt paper, and other miscellaneous tasks like cleaning the Machine and taking care of any errors like cash jams, paper jams, or card reader errors (while rare, they do need to be addressed).

The revenue sharing agreement often depends on the type of store where you plan to place your ATM. For instance, a retail store does not attract as many transactions as a casino. Therefore, the surcharge applied on ATMs may be higher. It's best to have some revenue projections in order to make the best decision when offering the store owner part of the revenue.

One thing you do need to consider is whether or not the store owner is bearing any costs related to the ATM. For instance, the store owner may agree to run the communication line via an internet connection.

Just make sure there are no surprises for the location owner. No one likes surprises, so be sure to discuss your responsibilities and his/hers and put it all in a site location agreement before you install the machine. This will ensure you can keep operating the ATM in the store for a long time to come.

What is a Site Location Agreement?

A Site Location Agreement is also known as the SLA. Once you have verbal approval from the owner, you need to obtain it in writing. No need to freak out here; the store owner probably wants to make the agreement binding and legal before you can install the machine in the store too. This is where the Site Location Agreement has to be completed.

As the name suggests, the site location agreement is a document that lists the terms and conditions between the two parties, (e.g. you and the store owner). Though the agreement depends on the things agreed upon between you and the store owner, there is a standard format you can follow. It usually lists 15 to 20 clauses, each of them entailing to your machine being installed in a retail store.

Most importantly, the site location agreement makes it clear that you are the owner of the ATM and the store is listed as the location. Among the other details included in the site location agreement are:

Placement of the machine

Responsibilities to be borne by each party

The length of time the agreement is valid for

Insurance, maintenance and other related issues

Any relevant terms and conditions agreed upon by the two parties are listed in the site location agreement. To put it simply, the site location agreement defines the roles and responsibilities for the store owner and the operator of the ATM machine, which you are. Make sure you discuss all of the details of the agreement in detail before signing on the dotted line. ATM Depot IADs can access their member area to access many custom forms and help videos, where you can download an SLA you can use or alter. If you choose another provider, be sure to ask if they offer a Site Location Agreement Template that you can alter for your use.

How to Talk to Location Owners and Negotiate a Deal?

Back when I was going door-to-door selling ATMs before placements were popular, I would walk into a liquor store, convenience store, or small grocery store with a piece of ½" or ¾" painted plywood cut to the same dimensions as the base of the ATM. This way, I knew exactly how much space I would need without breaking out a tape measure.

I would photo copy five $100 bills and tape them to one side of the plywood. Then I would walk the store and find a spot where I thought the ATM could do well and I would place the painted plywood on the floor.

When the counter person was not busy (never bother business owners during busy hours), I would walk up to them and say, "Excuse me, is the owner of the store available?" They would usually ask "why" or say "no." I would tell them that I found $500 on the floor and wanted to show the owner. Then a few different things would happen.

1. They would not believe me and ask me where.

    a. I would tell them I'd be happy to show the owner if he/she is here and, if not, I'd like to call the owner personally.

    b. If they would not give me the owner's phone number I would not give them a business card, but I would give them my phone number and ask them to have the owner call me. When he/she called, and he/she often did, I would tell him/her I didn't have time to talk to him/her at the moment, but I could call him/her back if he/she could be so kind as to give me his/her name and phone number. These days, with cell phones and caller ID, it's easier. Once I had the owner's contact information, he/she would go into my sales calls schedule, and I would try to make an in-person appointment.

2. If the owner was there, I would greet the owner, introduce myself, and get his/her name. Then I would show him/her the plywood on the floor with the photocopied $500. At first, he/she would think I'm trying to fool him/her, (but since it's a sales gimmick) I had to quickly go into my pitch.

   a. I would typically say, "Mr./Miss [Last name], I wanted to show you how I can find this $500 here every month. While I didn't really find $500 today, what I can put in place of this plywood is very real, and it would produce more than $500 in revenue for you every month. Would you be interested in getting $500 per month from this space?"

b. Then I would stop talking and see what he/she said.

c. He/She would almost always be curious as to what it was. Very rarely would he/she say, "no, I already have plans for that space."

d. When he/she said he/she might be interested, I would then ask him/her if now was a good time to go to his/her office for 5 – 10 minutes. If not, I would make an appointment to meet him/her within the next few days at a mutually convenient time.

e. Note that if he/she wanted to learn more right there, I needed to be prepared. I had a small notebook with some ATM brochures, a brief presentation, and my agreements. Sometimes I could close the deal right there; other times, it would take a few visits.

f. If after the presentation he/she wasn't sure or wasn't interested, I would thank him/her for his/her time but would be sure to ask if he/she had any other locations or if he/she had any friends or family with a store that could benefit from an ATM inside.

g. If I closed the deal, I would get the paperwork and then call him/her in a few days to make sure he/she had the power and communications line ready. Once he/she did, I would visit again to make sure and then schedule the delivery and installation.

h. Keep in mind: Back then, I was selling ATMs for hundreds of dollars per month on a five-year business lease. You're not selling the owner anything. You want to try to place your own ATM in the location. You are removing all of the owner's risk and giving him/her a reward. It's not going to make the owners $500 per month, but if it's a good location, it should be at least $100 from the ATM transactions, plus incremental sales from the extra cash in customer's hands, as well as the savings from reduced credit card usage fees.

It is important to make sure your proposal is a win-win for you and the location. You want to negotiate favorable terms and conditions for all involved parties. Since the store is providing you the space to install your ATM, the store owner might feel as though he/she deserves a larger share of the revenue without taking on any responsibilities. Never make a deal where both parties (you and the store owner) are not completely happy. No matter how badly you may want that location, there are other places if you can't strike an equitable deal.

This is why you have to know how to negotiate with the locations. In this regard, your ATM provider can help you out (ATMDepot can offer this type of help should you need it).

ATM providers have the experience of installing hundreds of machines before they install yours. As a result, they can help you to get the best terms and conditions that suit your needs. You should make use of their expertise and experience to get the terms you want.

However, make sure you don't overdo the negotiation phase. Don't get carried away in the process and try to get everything in your favor. You have to allow some leeway to the store owner else he/she might lose interest in the agreement and cancel it. It has to be a win-win for all parties. If you ensure both parties can make money and the deal works for everyone, you will have a long and prosperous relationship.

If you have some experience negotiating terms with locations, give it a try. If you don't have any experience, be sure to finish reading this book, as it will go a long way towards helping you find your feet in the ATM business. You don't need experience to negotiate with locations; it's okay to learn as you go. All the location owner can do is say, 'no, thank you.' Each subsequent try will get you closer to a deal. Should you need them, telephone scripts with answers to objections can be obtained in the member's area on ATMDepot.com.

I suggest you start out by talking to people you already know who might have a good location if you know retailers, or talk to friends who might know of a good location for an ATM. You can also call new business listings to make appointments. There are many good new business directories and listing resources, such as publications and lists you can purchase.

If you are a frequent patron of an establishment you think would be a good place for your ATM, talk to the owner.

Remember, no one likes a sales pitch. It's much easier to state a problem many similar retailers have, since you have a solution. One main problem for most retailers is the cost of accepting credit cards. A friendly opening line if you are in the store buying something with your credit card is to make a comment that accepting credit cards is getting more and more expensive and more complicated. Then listen to what the counter person says.

You can then let them know that while you're not in the merchant processing business and you're not selling anything, that you help small business owners reduce their credit card fees with no cost, and you can explain it in just a few minutes. Then ask for the owner's contact information so you can pass that info along.

That usually gets you the owner's name and phone number so you can call him/her. Be sure to get the name of the person at the store that gave you the contact information so you can use it when you call the owner.

Another approach is to casually ask if there is an ATM close by, and then ask if other customers ask about an ATM. Depending on their answer, ask the counter person (bar tender, waiter/waitress, etc) for the owner's contact information. Let him/her know you have a solution for people who ask about an ATM.

If he/she is hesitant to give you that information, ask if there is a manager available or what would be a good time to visit when the owner is on-site. The key to this visit is to get the contact info for the decision maker so you can talk to him/her to see if there is any interest. Sometimes, bar or nightclub owners are not there, and they have trusted managers.

Whether you have to visit again to speak to a decision maker or to get the owner's contact information when you do reach them, be sure to let him/her know you are a frequent customer.

Let him/her know that (name of employee) mentioned that customers often ask if an ATM is available or close by. Then ask if he/she has ever thought of adding an ATM in his/her establishment, especially if he/she is sending customers across the street or down the block to the (fill in the name of the place he/she tells customers to go).

Be sure to approach him/her as a patron or business person, not as a sales person (if you are a sales person). Let him/her know you're a frequent shopper and like his/her business. If you are speaking with him/her in person, you don't want to make this a casual conversation. Be sure to have a pen and paper or your smartphone handy and collect his/her contact information so you can schedule a mutually convenient time to meet in his/her office to sit down and explain all of the details.

You can let him/her know you help businesses get ATMs for free and would be interested in putting one in his/her business at no cost. Depending on his/her level of interest, you can even show him/her where you think a good location for the ATM is.

Obviously, before you do that, make sure you have already scoped out the premises and have a good idea as to the location for the placement of an ATM.

Let him/her know that all you need is one square foot of floor space; don't go into too many details at this point.

At any point, if he/she is interested when you are first talking, or if you are speaking with him/her over the phone, let him/her know you would like to meet with him/her to discuss the opportunity at a mutually convenient time in his/her office. Then ask if mornings, afternoons, or evenings are the best time for him/her to meet with you. Then make a real appointment.

Once you have a firm appointment and his/her undivided attention, you will know he/she is seriously interested. Then you can talk about the details. Include how he's/she's going to make more money having an ATM and that it can lower credit card costs, increase impulse spending, and offer a small share of the surcharge (you can start with $1.00 after the first 50 transactions, or anything you want). Be prepared with an SLA and close the deal.

Locations That Applied for a Liquor License

Installing an ATM machine in a liquor store or any other adult location where liquor is served is typically a great location. Note that some states have passed legislation restricting the use of EBT cards in ATMs in liquor stores. EBT (Electronic Benefits Transfer) is basically the government welfare network. If you get government assistance, your debit card uses the EBT network and, therefore, won't allow transactions in some of these locations. This is not necessarily a bad thing, since most EBT cards can't be surcharged anyway. But if the liquor store owner asks, you'll need to know this information.

There is no doubt that installing an ATM in a liquor store will prove to be quite lucrative. Generally, ATM businesses are able to place a higher surcharge fee on ATMs installed in liquor stores or establishments serving liquor. There is a good chance that you will see a huge number of customers, particularly if you have selected the liquor store carefully.

We've also seen higher transactions in liquor stores in undesirable neighborhoods if the machine dispenses $10s instead of $20s. During your due diligence in calculating the estimated number of daily customers, if the store is in a restrictive welfare state, be sure to ask the owner for his estimate on how many of those patrons are on government assistance. This way, you can back those out of your calculations.

Locations Going Through Change of Ownership

Generally, site location agreements are drawn up for a period of three to five years. Some store owners don't like long agreements; however, as the ATM owner, you want the longest possible term for your agreements, as you certainly don't want to have to remove your ATM if it's making money (or, worse, is proving it's a great business and then having the store owner purchase his/her own ATM from a competitor). This means that the store owner and the operator agree to have the machine running in the store for the agreed-upon term. There is, however, a chance that the business owner relocates or sells the store before the end of your agreement. What happens then? If the owner relocates to, perhaps, expand the store or get a better location, and you've established a good relationship, he/she will most likely ask you to follow him/her to the new location. That is the easiest thing to do.

However, it may not be feasible for you if he/she moves farther away than you're willing to travel. Also, the business might be shutting down the location because he/she is shutting down for good. In either case, you are the one who has to relocate and bear the hassles and costs associated with the move. If he/she is selling the location, your SLA should have a provision that transfers rights to the new owner. Make sure the previous owner introduces you to the new owner and helps you transition if the store is being sold.

This is why it is important that you discuss the business' future plans with the owner when creating the SLA. If he/she plans to move soon, it may or may not be a good idea for you to install a machine there.

Even if the business didn't plan to relocate but has to because of circumstances, the site location agreement states that the owner and operator of the machine be notified well in advance. Generally speaking, the location will have to inform you at least 30 days before the intended move. You can also negotiate and get him/her to increase the notice period so you get to know about the relocation a little earlier.

In case the ownership is changing, you can get in touch with the new owner to discover whether or not he/she would be interested in having an ATM on the premises. Since the machine has already been installed and people know about it, the business owner has nothing to lose from continuing to have the machine there. In that case, you are in luck, as you don't have to move the machine from one place to another.

However, if the new owner is not interested in an ATM machine being there, you may end up having to relocate. Again, the site location agreement will guide you as to the responsibilities of the previous location in such a case. You can negotiate to have the cost of relocation included in the site location agreement. We suggest you try to negotiate a split or flat rate fee if forced to move through no fault of your own.

Programming & Installation

There is no doubt that programming and installation is one of the key stages of setting up an ATM business. Your machines have to be programmed to be used by customers during the setup. You must ensure that they are installed properly, meaning they are secured to the floor and adhere to ADA requirements (which include the ability for wheelchair access and proper decals). With that in mind, let's look at how this process is completed.

How Is An ATM Programmed?

Most ATMs are shipped from the factory and typically need to be programmed during installation on-site, as they are made to order, based on the hardware selected. Sometimes, you can purchase a standard pre-configured machine or a refurbished machine (when available) if you need it faster. The good news is that these ATM machines can often be programmed before shipping, which means when you receive them, they are ready to use. While that is great and saves on installation fees and time, there can be additional fees for shipping or handling. They will still require to be installed at the location, which includes securing it to the floor, connecting power, and establishing communications prior to use.

Most ATM providers require programming to be completed by professional field technicians. Typical fees can range from $295 –$450 (average of $350), depending on the location and several other factors. However, a less expensive option offered by only a few companies is call-in or scheduled programming and training by phone. We find that once you install and program a few ATMs, you will have the process down and can do them yourself without any assistance if you so desire.

If you are technically savvy and don't mind doing some of the programming yourself, and if you work with ATMDepot.com, you can arrange for phone-in training and programming or access videos in our member area. However, since programming is critical, if you are not that technically savvy, we do recommend you go with an experienced professional for your first one and take notes so you can opt for the call-in programming and do it yourself for your subsequent machines if you are so inclined.

Programming involves setting up the machine to be used by customers. Everything, from the picture that shows on the screen when the machine is not in use to the denomination of bills that are to be used in the ATM, has to be programmed. In other words, an ATM machine cannot be used until it has been properly programmed. This is why qualified professionals program the machines for you. It's not really that difficult once you know what's needed, but it can be time-consuming if you've never done it before.

How Is the Machine Installed?

There is a proper process that needs to be followed when the machine is being installed:

> Before securing the ATM to the floor, be sure to select an area that will meet all of the ADA requirements for space in front of the ATM (enough for wheelchair access). Also, be sure the ATM will be level. Once you secure the ATM to the floor, an uneven surface

can warp the sides or leave room for crowbars underneath. The surface on which the machine is to be installed should be flat and level.

The machine has to be securely bolted to the floor. There are pre-drilled holes in the base plate on the inside of the ATM. You or your installer would place the ATM where it goes on the floor, mark the holes with a permanent marker, then move the ATM and, using a center punch, punch the center of the marks. Then using a hammer drill with a ½" concrete bit, you or the installer would drill the holes in the floor at least 3.75" – 4" deep. Since concrete slabs are typically 4" thick, it's important not to drill too far through, but deep enough for the bolts. Once the holes are drilled, the ATM is moved back into place. Once the ATM is in place, special concrete anchors called "Red Heads" are then hammered into the holes. We recommend Anchors that are ½" x 4.25." It's important to note that you must place the Red Head through the hole in the base plate of the ATM, then into the concrete. It's also important to note that before hammering the anchor deep into the hole you drilled, place the washer and nut onto the threaded end. If you hammer the threaded end prior to placing the nut on first, you risk damaging the threads, making it difficult if not impossible to put the nut on after.

Once the ATM is properly secured to the floor, it is plugged into a power outlet. A 110V/AC outlet is required for this purpose. We recommend a dedicated circuit, but if that is not possible, be sure to use a surge protector with at least a 1000 joule rating.

Lastly, the machine has to be connected to an analog phone line (new digital telephone lines do not work well), an Internet connection (if the ATM is capable of Internet processing), or a wireless communication device. The best approach is to use a separate dedicated wireless device or the location's high-speed internet connection if it's reliable.

The average ATM machine weighs between 160 and 250 pounds. In this regard, it can be said that the machine isn't heavier than a large safe. This is why it's important to properly secure it to the floor.

Are There Any Installation Options?

You can do the installation on your own, hire a professional ATM technician to do the job for you, or work with your ATM provider to coordinate the installation. You have to ensure the installation is done thoroughly and properly. Hiring a professional does cost a few bucks, but it ensures the machine is installed perfectly.

What Is ATM Management and How Is It Different From an ATM Placement?

You can outsource the entire process and management of installing, maintaining and operating the ATM you have purchased to a service. This kind of agreement is known as ATM management. Rather than operating the ATM on your own, you hire an ATM management company to do it for you. The company you select will charge fees for each service you wish to have managed. If you purchase the ATM, you can have the management company load cash, handle maintenance, and all of the other functions, or just some of them. It's up to you which parts you wish to have managed.

What you get in return with complete ATM management is absolute comfort. You can rest assured that all things related to the installation and operation of your machines is under control. You only have to inform the company where the machine is to be installed, and they will do it all for you.

The services offered will vary from company to company. If you want to hire a company for this purpose, you can discuss your needs with your ATM provider.

An ATM Placement is typically an arrangement where an ATM company or IAD would place an ATM in a location and own and operate all aspects of the ATM machine. The location proprietor would get a small percentage of the revenue generated from the ATM for letting the IAD place the ATM in the location. If you are considering investing in ATMs as a business, you would be the IAD, and you would typically want to find locations that want placements. You would then work with your ATM provider to help you operate your ATMs profitably and to select the right locations.

What's Available?

To ensure the success of your ATM business, you'll have to invest in high-quality ATM machines. There is no dearth of options when it comes to buying ATM machines, which is both a good thing and a bad thing. The good thing is that you have plenty of options to choose from, ensuring you can get exactly what you are looking for.

The bad thing is that with such a variety to explore, one can end up feeling confused and making the wrong choice. When starting your business, the last thing you would want is to select substandard ATM machines. The best option is to stick to the best machines available at the present time. A few of them are highlighted below:

The Best Machines Currently

Hyosung Halo ATM

The Halo ATM is named so for a reason: there is an actual halo of light around the pin pad. The color of the light changes frequently, giving the machine an attractive and alluring appearance. This is perhaps one ATM machine that can attract passersby and get them to withdraw cash. Needless to say, many ATM businesses using Hyosung Halo ATMs are more successful than others when using this feature. The lights in the Halo can be configured in a variety of ways and colors depending upon your needs and the location atmosphere.

Not only is the 'halo' an attractive feature, the machine has a 10-inch LCD screen, which is also quite captivating. The screen can be optimized to add graphics. The operating system for the Hyosung Halo ATM is Windows, which is a proven mainstream standard for ATMs. Be wary of any ATM that is running proprietary operating systems these days.

This ATM is EMV (European MasterCard Visa) option ready as a standard. Upgrading the card reader is an easy option from the factory, which I personally recommend you order, and it shouldn't be difficult to field-upgrade either. It is expected that all ATM machines in the US would have to be EMV-enabled in the not-too-distant future. Buying the Hyosung Halo ATM for your business enables you to get a head start.

There are a host of upgrades and optional hardware you can also purchase for this ATM machine. The machine itself is not that heavy, weighing in at around 176 lbs, but the overall size is small, fitting nicely into tight spaces and not using much room where floor space is at a premium. Plus, it's incredibly durable. Since prices on ATMs change often, we will not be quoting pricing in this book. Simply contact your ATM provider for up-to-date pricing on any ATM models. However, at the time of publicatio,n you should be able to get this machine nicely configured with the EMV upgrade, an electronic lock with delivery, and installation for under $2500.00.

Genmega G1900

The Genmega G1900 is a no-frills ATM machine that is perfect for any professional ATM business. This machine is cost-effective to purchase, own, and operate. Since you don't have to make a huge investment for buying this machine, you can start turning a profit quicker than you would through other, more expensive ATM machines.

In many ways, the Genmega G1900 has features and design similar to the Hantle 1700. In terms of security, this is among the most secure ATM machines you can purchase. It may not have the visual appeal of the Hyosung Halo, but it will serve your purpose nevertheless, and it is often a great option when using it in a conventional installation.

Hantle Mini Bank 1700W or Genmega G2500

The Hantle Mini Bank 1700W pictured right or the Genmega G2500 pictured below with a shark skip wrap is a machine you should consider if you intend to set up an ATM at a busy location. The unique aspect of these ATM machines is that you can install one, two, or four cassette options. This means that there is a considerable amount of cash in the machine at all times. Even with constant withdrawals, the machine doesn't run out of cash anytime soon. If you plan to have professional vaulting or multiple cassettes in a traditional environment, this is a great option.

Multiple cassettes make it easier to operate, since you don't have to reload the cassette as often, but the difference in price may or may not be worthwhile. You would have to factor in all of the associated costs, including traveling to the ATM, to see if the numbers pan out. Keep in mind that you can space out your visits to the ATM location (if you load it yourself). Instead of going once a week for a single cassette machine, you may go once or twice a month. The capability to hold multiple cassettes also means that the machine can be programmed to dispense different denominations.

The design of the machine is top-of-the-line. It looks very much like a modern ATM machine (which it is). While these machines typically come standard with a 7-inch or 8-inch color LCD screen with a high-resolution display, you can usually upgrade to a large screen if necessary.

These are just some of the newest ATM machines currently available. Of course, these are merely the tip of the iceberg. There are many other options you can explore. Keep the features of these leading machines in mind so that you have an idea of what to look for in a high-quality ATM machine. After all, buying the best possible machines for your business is a must.

What Machines to Avoid

With so many new American Disability Act (ADA) requirements over the last few years, we've seen an abundance of used or outdated ATMs come on the used market. Unfortunately, these are typically purchased by unsuspecting new ATM operators looking for a deal, and they unknowingly get duped.

These old ATMs (maybe not as old as the one pictured left; this was taken by me in 1994 when we first started in the business) are nothing but boat anchors or spare parts for dying breeds. Many of these ATMs can't even legally be run in the USA any longer.

Some of these ATMs include older or vintage ATM models by Tidel and Triton. Make sure the manufacturer date of any ATM you look at is less than a few years old. Don't buy any ATM's that are over 5 years old. I would stay away from Tidel, Diebold, and NCR ATMs altogether, as they can be problematic. While Triton ATMs are wonderful, they have been around a long time, so there are some outdated ones that show up on auction sites. If you are considering a used Triton, be sure to find out the model and the year it was manufactured. The Triton Mako cannot be installed any longer, and many of the older models have been retired. Speak with your ATM company about processing for any older machines before you buy one.

All ATMs have a manufactured date. If the ATM was manufactured prior to 2012, it most likely needs an ADA upgrade. Which, by the time you pay for the ATM, ship it, refurbish it, and upgrade it you could have purchased a new ATM with a parts and labor warranty. When unsure, please call your ATM company and, if they don't know, call ATMDepot.com.

ADA Guidelines

The American with Disabilities Act (ADA) has proposed a few guidelines regarding ATMs. Any new ATM installed after March 15, 2012 has to be in compliance with the rules and regulations outlined in the ADA guidelines. The purpose is to make it easier for disabled people to use ATMs. The law applies to each ATM your business owns.

There is no way for you to get around these requirements. You have to comply with them in order to operate your ATM business legally. If you already own an ATM, you have to make sure that it is in line with these requirements.

Keep in mind that if the ATM provider gets named in a lawsuit and is sued because compliance is not met, the merchant (location where the ATM is installed), most likely, has a responsibility and a contractual agreement to indemnify the provider in the litigation. This is another reason that the ATM paperwork is so important.

Listed below are the current ADA guidelines for ATMs:

Height & Reach

To ensure consumers can easily access input controls, an ATM's reach, meaning the height of the upper most function key, must be no higher than 48 inches from the ground. This was lowered from 54" in the past few years, and it is possible some older ATMs are still active and just haven't been upgraded yet. Merchants and IADs sometimes push the limits and risk an ADA lawsuit by waiting longer than they should. It is important to note that if the live touch-command areas on the ATM screen are higher than the function keys, the graphic area containing the touch commands must be lowered to the required height for the unit to be compliant.

Most freestanding retail ATM machines do not have touchscreens yet and would, therefore, comply. However, as technology advances and future ADA updates are made, you need to make sure you are working with an ATM company that will keep you abreast of the trends. Drive-thru ATMs need not follow this regulation.

ATM Area

There should be floor space of 30 x 48 inches (10 sq. ft.) in front of the ATM to comply with the ADA wheelchair access guidelines.*

ADA Compliance – Merchant Responsibility

The new ATM - ADA requirements pertain to the open floor space in front of an ATM. This is the responsibility of the property manager or merchant, regardless of the arrangement made with the Independent ATM deployer or another ATM provider. It is the merchant's responsibility to ensure the proper legal requirements for wheelchair access.

The minimum clear floor or ground space required for accommodating a single, stationary wheelchair and occupant is 30 in by 48 in (760 mm by 1220 mm).

Source:
http://www.ada.gov/regs2010/2010ADAStandards/2010ADAstandards.htm

Route

The entrance to the ATM must have a clear route leading up to it. This is to allow easy access to wheelchair-bound individuals.

Speech-Enabled Functionality – aka Voice Guidance

Every ATM machine in the US is required to be speech-enabled for visually impaired customers. A 3.5mm female jack has to be installed in the ATM to allow the customers to use headphones.

Speech output is considered by the ADA to be an auxiliary aid or service, so implementation is required unless doing so would create an undue burden or expense. Make sure when you purchase an ATM that it is a late model and meets this requirement, as well as the others below.

Braille Instructions

The speech-enabled ATMs need to have instructions in Braille for visually-impaired customers to allow them to activate the voice feature. Most ATM companies include a welcome kit that includes a Braille decal; however, most manufacturers have since included Braille on the machine surface. Since Voice guidance can change depending on the ATM, if you do receive a decal from your ATM company, be sure to place it on the machine located near the Audio Jack.

Display Screen

The display screen of the machine has to be visible from 40 inches above the center of the floor in front of it. The font to be used for the text has to be San Serif. The font should be in a color that contrasts with the background and must be at least 3/16 inch high. Since the ATM manufacturers know these guidelines, you would not need to be concerned about them, but you should be aware of them.

Function Keys

The keys on the machine should be in a color different from the surface. The manufacturers know these guidelines and design the keys to contrast visually from their background surfaces.

Input Devices

Customers should be able to discern the input devices. For this, the keys should be raised above the surface, which all ATM manufacturers are aware.

Numeric Keys

The numeric layout of the keypad can be in ascending or descending order. The 'Enter' key should have a raised circle. The 'Clear' key should have a raised left arrow, indicating that pressing the key would erase what has been typed. The 'Add Value' and 'Decrease Value' keys should have plus and minus signs respectively.

In case a location has more than one machine, the one most accessible from the entrance has to comply with the ADA guidelines. If there is one ATM inside a location and one outside, both of them have to be compliant. Only drive-thru ATMs are exempt from these guidelines. Also, they apply to all existing and new ATMs without exception.

In case your ATMs don't comply with the law, you might have to bear a civil penalty, which could be as high as $55,000 even for the first offense. The amount simply doubles for each subsequent offense.

You can ask your ATM provider to help you set up ATMs that are compliant with the ADA regulations so that you don't have to bear any legal hassle in the future. Also, providing services to disabled customers ensures that your machines get more transactions.

All ATMs shipped to the USA for retail sale must have this configuration, but some of the older ATMs have plastic keys and may not have the latest VEPP keypad. Since this is the ADA section, we are not going to discuss Network requirements here, as that will be discussed in another section.

ATM Security

What's the Difference between Dial Combo Lock and e-Lock?

A dial combo lock is the typical lock that comes on most safes and has tumblers where you turn the dial left 3x, then right 2x, then left 1x, then back again to open the safe. These locks are fairly standard and have been used for centuries.

The pros to these locks are that they are inexpensive and come standard on ATMs when you buy one. The cons to these locks are the combo is difficult to change and requires a change key that comes with the ATM. They take longer to open and, if you are loading an ATM during a busy day when the store is open, people can see what you are up to as it takes a few minutes to perfect.

Since a dial combo comes standard on most ATM machines when you purchase them, there is no additional cost.

An e-Lock is an electronic lock upgrade. If you order a new ATM with one, depending on the model, the upgrades are usually only $50 - $100 and installed at the factory. If you wait to order one later or buy a used ATM with a standard dial combo and want to upgrade it to an e-lock, the costs can be $150 plus a locksmith or an ATM field technician service call.

E-Locks are a simple touch keypad combo that looks similar to a telephone keypad. They take less than a few seconds to enter the correct combo to open your ATM.

Pros: Easy, fast access to the ATM.

Cons: Cost a little extra.

I highly recommend spending a few extra dollars if you plan to order new ATMs for your ATM business. When you consider the total investment and the amount of time and hassle an e-lock saves, it's a no-brainer. If you plan to load several ATMs in one day, getting stuck for 10 –30 minutes opening a dial combo lock can make a huge difference in your day.

Lastly a Kaba Mas or Cencon Lock is an electronic lock that includes the ability to assign special digital keys so you can perform a security audit. These locks are required when hiring an armored carrier for vault cash services. These locks tend to cost $500 - $600 dollars each.

Should I Install a Camera?

Adding a camera to your ATM location is one of the easiest ways to secure it. Not only are cameras inconspicuous, they provide a real-time feed of the location at which your ATM has been installed. Nothing deters a thief as much as being caught on camera. Having their face recorded on video means they will get implicated if caught. The job of the law enforcement authorities is easier once they can see the face.

The only reason people are apprehensive about adding cameras to their ATM location is the cost. Cameras can be a tad expensive to purchase and, unless the machine has started generating revenue, making a further investment can be a problem for some new investors. That being said, it is another effective way to keep your ATM secure, so it is a worthwhile investment.

So, what you can do is to get a couple of Web-ready cameras. We typically install a 3rd-party camera system at our ATM locations, a 2-camera system from Costco or Amazon with one facing the ATM and one facing the entrance to the location. Then we add decals and on-screen graphics that say, "Smile, you're on camera." This does a good job of deterring the wannabe thief.

How often do ATMs get stolen?

Not all ATM robberies are reported, but the percentage is very low based on the number of ATMs in the USA. Most thieves know that there is not much cash in freestanding retail ATMs, they are bolted to the ground, and have a UL 291 security rating. Most thieves find it's not worth the risk these days. It's also easy to add security such as cameras, alarms, and other security measures. Plus, you can always opt to purchase insurance for your equipment as well as the cash for a nominal monthly fee. For example, as of this writing, you can get coverage for up to $2000 in equipment coverage plus up to $2500 in cash for about $12 per month.

Additional Security Measures

Apart from adding the locks and cameras, there are a couple of other security measures you can put into place:

Make sure the space around the machine is well-lit. The risk of theft and robbery is reduced when there are lights shining all around. People also feel safer when using an ATM that is well-lit.

Install an alarm at the location if the location doesn't already have one. Most thieves will avoid any store or location that is well-lit and has an alarm.

Whenever possible, install ATMs inside, away from large windows or glass doors.

Try to select locations that have long open hours; if they are open 24 hours; that is the best type of location.

If you're a store owner with an ATM, and you or your managers are on-site, you can also make it a point to remove the cash from the machine every night if you wish. This is pretty much the same thing you would do with your cash register.

Security is an extremely important issue when it comes to an ATM business. While there is limited risk, you should also make customers feel comfortable. Only then can you expect your business to grow and deliver the kind of profits you expect. Keep these security measures in mind, and you are good to go. If you want to protect your investment with insurance, you can do that also. While this is not a security measure, it can give you peace of mind if that is something you need.

ATM Screens

In this chapter, we will be going over some useful information related to ATM screens. A majority of ATM business owners don't know about the influence the size of the screen or a color screen has on their business. This is why they don't pay much attention to the type of screen they are selecting. Therefore, it is important that you go through this chapter carefully.

Benefits of Color Screens

Most ATM business owners fail to make the most of color screens on their machines. Most modern ATM machines come equipped with color screens regardless of the brand you purchase. It is a standard feature on many of today's ATMs, since the price of LED and LCD panels has dropped. You typically don't have to pay extra to get a color-screen-equipped ATM. There are numerous benefits of color screens that most ATM operators don't realize and, hence, miss out on. Let's go over some of them:

Add a color image that catches the eye and captures the attention of the customers. Having a store logo or custom welcome screen on your ATM is more professional and appealing to customers. We've done several studies; ATMs with a color welcome screen definitely have higher usage. People feel more connected when the image on the ATM looks like the surroundings or instills confidence about using your ATM, particularly to individuals who spend most of their time in the vicinity and are likely to use your machine regularly.

You can have advertisement screens rotate in with the welcome and transaction screens. It can be an ad for the location where the machine is located offering a special deal to ATM users, you can sell advertising space to local businesses, or you can even advertise your own business to get more ATM locations.

'Brand' the machines you buy for your business by having your logo rotate in on the welcome screen when the machines are idle. This is a great way to signify your brand identity and show that the machine is operated by your company.

At the end of the day, it is up to you, the owner, to decide what you want to do with the color screen. Keep in mind that you have a few possibilities to explore, so make the choice accordingly. We don't know of anyone other than ATMDepot.com that offers a free custom welcome screen with each ATM location. Most ATM providers charge $95 per screen to create them, but you can easily create them yourself, as your ATM provider should provide the necessary specifications for your ATM equipment type.

Another great benefit of color screens on your ATM is that most of the modern ones have a rotating screen. This means that you can add multiple images. The image will then rotate at an interval you set (usually from 5 seconds to 30 seconds) and a different image will appear at each interval. The best thing about the rotating screens is that they are eye-catching. You can capture the attention of the people passing by your ATM.

If you are the location owner, and you run your own ATM, make sure that your ATM shows special offers or promotions on the screen. For instance, you may advertise your 'Happy Hour' to passersby. In other words, the color screen will help you to educate your customers about your business. Many ATMs have a 10" screen available now, which is the size of a large iPad or tablet. This makes for a nice presentation and can provide users and passersby with information where they might just make a purchase.

So, as you can see, there are numerous benefits of color screens for an ATM business. Since color screens are a standard feature, there is no doubt that you will buy one that already has a color screen. The main purpose of highlighting these benefits is to inform you of the various benefits you can gain through them if you use them properly.

Different Screen Sizes Available

Apart from having a color screen on your machines, it is also important that you know about the different screen sizes available. Only then can you choose the one most appropriate based on the type of customers you are likely to attract. When it comes to screen sizes, there are several sizes, but three main options available to you:

1. 7" TFT LCD Screen (Hantle 1700W)
2. 8" LCD (Triton) & 8" TFT LCD (Genmega)
3. 10.1 – 10.4" (Hyosung & Genmega)

All four brands mentioned here provide color screens, so, regardless of the screen size you choose, you can buy ATMs that have color screens. The prices of all of these models vary, but are typically comparable, as is the technology used in them. The biggest screen you can buy is a 15", but that would be for a thru-the-wall ATM, not a freestanding machine. The current largest screen for a freestanding machine with a comparable price of all four brands listed is the 10.1". You can upgrade some other equipment to a 10.2" Wide LCD Touchscreen, but it does not come standard.

While it can be confusing to determine the screen size you need, the general rule is to install the biggest screen you can afford for the type of location. If you are going to install your ATM into a high-end night club or other venue where it may not be well-lit, or your ATM will be competing for attention with flashing colored dance lights or other forms of advertising, the larger and brighter the screen, the better. Keep your graphics bright and use whites, greens and yellows in the images versus blacks, reds and browns, as these tend to make the screen darker and harder to see. If you're installing the ATM in a not-so-great area or in a parking garage, for example, and people have to walk by it to get out of the store or building, then you can opt for a smaller screen if the machine is less expensive. The difference in price of a larger screen is not always that much, so always go for the bigger screen if you can. If the bigger screen attracts even just a few more people per month to use the ATM, it will pay for itself in no time.

How to Get Graphics onto Your ATM:

The instructions you have to follow for uploading your graphics to the machine differ from model to model. This is why you need to be mindful of the fact that your graphics need to be in the proper format and neatly saved into different folders. As far as the process of uploading is concerned, you can do it through a USB stick (i.e. flash drive) or an SD card, depending on how your ATM is equipped. Your ATM provider should be able to walk you through doing this the first time or may offer video tutorials on how this is done properly to avoid frustration.

If you find it difficult to come up with the appropriate graphics for your machines, you can get in touch with a professional to help you out. Not only will they design the graphics, keeping in mind your brand image, but will also ensure the files are saved in the proper format. From there on, you need to only upload the files, which can be easily done by following the instructions provided to you. You can create them yourself, but you need not spend more than $50 - $100 per screen on graphics.

If you choose to work with ATMDepot.com, we can create the graphics for you. You can discuss your needs with us, and we will design the appropriate screens for you. We will save them in the proper format to ensure they run smoothly and you don't face any problems later on.

Coming back to the point, you can choose any screen size you want. That being said, the bigger the screen, the easier the machine is to see and use!

Loading and Reloading the ATM

How Much Cash Do I Need To Load?

The amount of cash you need to load into the machine depends on a few factors:

1. The type of cassette that is installed will determine the maximum cash limits; however, it is rare to ever need to fill the machines to capacity. There are two types of cassettes, and some machines can handle multiple cassettes for extremely busy locations, but most machines you see in retailers are single-cassette ATMs.

   a. A fixed note cassette is exactly as it sounds. The cassette does not come out of the ATM and is refilled in place, similar to a napkin holder where you slide back a pressure plate and insert the cash. Fixed note cassettes typically hold 800– 1000 notes.

b. The second type of cassette is a removable cassette. Removable cassettes typically hold 1000– 1700 notes, which, again, is more than enough for busy locations.

2. You would not use brand new notes (bills) in your ATM, as they tend to stick together and are not good for ATM use. Your bank should give you ATM currency (which is recycled currency) in banded packets of $1,000 if you are getting $10s or $2,000 if you are getting $20s. A typical fixed cassette will hold approximately $14,000 (in $20s), which should be more than enough cash if you are loading your ATM weekly.

3. How busy is the location? Meaning, when you determined the location was a good ATM candidate, what criteria did you use? When you know what your estimated transactions are, you can determine the minimum cash requirements. Let's say you calculated the ATM would produce 5 transactions daily (more on how to estimate this later in the book). If the average

withdrawal is $80, the machine will need at least $400 per day. How often you want to load it will determine how much you need to load. If you want to go every 10 days, in this example, we would suggest you load at least $3,500 - $4,000 and then monitor it using real-time online monitoring (your ATM company should provide this). You can check the online monitoring system as often as you like to see the cash run rate so you can adjust the cash amounts until you get the timing down, but it's easy to use the ATM alert system and get text messages on your phone when the ATM is running low. You don't want to set the alerts for too low of a balance; otherwise, it can run out. We suggest at least $1 – 2$ days at the current run rate as the low balance alert. You can start with a $500 alert to play it safe before it runs out of cash.

4. We recommend loading at least $2,000 to start with, depending on how busy the location can be. If you don't have that much cash to start with, you can always start with less, even as little as $500, but remember, if your machine runs out of cash, you're out of business. The funds are put back into your account the next business

day, so you can withdraw those funds and put them back into the machine. However, you don't want to run out of cash on weekends, as banks are not open. You can use your own bank's ATM in an emergency to get more cash for your ATM on weekends, but the max you can typically get would be $300 or $500, which is fine unless you have a busy ATM. Also remember that since banks are not open on weekends or holidays, the cash dispensed from your ATM Friday – Sunday is put back into your account the following Monday. Keep in mind bank holidays that land on a Friday or Monday.

If you need help determining the amount of cash for a specific location, your ATM company should be able to help you to determine what's best.

Who Loads the ATM?

As the owner of the machine, you can load the ATM yourself, have the store owner load cash, hire a vaulting service, or even pay for armored car services.

The most profitable way to operate your ATM business is to load the cash yourself. It is a simple process as you can see from this how to load cash video on YouTube. While this video shows an older style cassette and dispenser, it's still similar to most models, other than the dispenser rotation.

If you have less than a couple dozen ATMs, you can create a weekly, bi-weekly, or 3x per month route to load cash. We recommend alternating load days and times so you don't fall into a pattern that nosy employees or someone else notices. We also have some ATM operators that hire off-duty police or plain clothes security to accompany them a few times a month if they are venturing into neighborhoods where they are uncomfortable. If you're a frequent customer of the establishment where you have the ATM installed (which is how many ATM owners start out), it's perfectly normal for you to visit the location often. You can even make arrangements with store owners or building managers to load the ATM during closed or off-hours, and many store owners let ATM operators load cash in their back office; this is where a removable cassette comes in handy.

If you have a business partner or trusted employees, you can delegate the cash-loading service. You can also wait until the machines start running low on cash (using SMS alerts) and just load them whenever you need to instead of having a specific route. You decide when you want to load the cash and who is going to load it. So, as far as the question of who is going to load the ATM is concerned, the owner has to decide.

Another popular method to load cash is to have the store owner do it daily. Typically, store owners would load about $800 - $1,000 prior to opening each day and remove any remaining funds when closing. They balance the ATM just like a cash register, except the ATM is only one denomination, so it's much easier. The only issue is when the store owner forgets, is lazy that day, gets sick, or doesn't have enough cash flow that day to load cash; then, you are basically out of business until they load the ATM again. You may also have to share more of the surcharge income with the store owner for loading cash, which reduces your profits.

Another popular method is to hire a vaulting service or to pay for armored car services. Both of these options can cost more than you are willing to share, so you should be sure that you have a busy ATM or that you want to outsource this function before committing to these options. However, this does open up many more possibilities for placing ATMs further from where you live.

Most ATM operators start by loading the ATM themselves and, if the ATM is very busy or if they have too many ATMs to load, then contracting out the vaulting is a way to grow your business. Vaulting or armored services can cost between $150 and $400 or more, depending on how busy the ATM is, how much cash is needed and how often it needs to be filled.

Pros and Cons of Fixed Note Cassettes

As mentioned above, there are two types of ATM cassettes. First, we are going to go over fixed note cassettes. The name clearly suggests that this type of cassette is fixed into the machine and cannot be removed. You have to load the cash into the machine where it is bolted down. Let's look at the pros and cons of fixed note cassettes.

Pros

ATMs with fixed note cassettes are a little cheaper as compared to the ones with removable cassettes.

The capacity of a typical fixed note cassette is still plenty (800 - 1,000 notes depending on the manufacturer) for a busy location.

You don't have to remove any components or parts from the ATM to reload the cash. Simply open up the cassette and insert the cash.

Very quick to load: Insert key, lift up door, insert cash, lock cassette.

Cons

You have to load the cash where the ATM is (usually in a busy area). You cannot take the cassette to a secure location where you would feel safe loading the cash.

Typically smaller capacity for both cassette and reject tray. If the cassette is fixed, the reject tray is also not removable.

Typical Fixed Note Cassette Specs:

CDU Type: Drawer type (fixed)

Maintenance: Front Service Type

Cassette Capacity: 800 - 1,000 Notes

Reject Capacity: Reject Box: 100 Notes

Dispense Speed: 2 Notes / sec

Note Pick up: Friction

Power Supply: DC24V, 5V

Dimension: 250mm*220mm*360mm(W*H*D)

Weight: < 7kg

Pros and Cons of Removable Cassettes

You can see from the name that removable cassettes can be removed from the machine to be reloaded. This is what makes them different from fixed note cassettes. Let's go over the pros and cons of removable cassettes as well.

Pros

The most obvious pro is that you can remove the cassette from the ATM and take it to a safe and discreet location for loading the cash. This gives you greater security when dealing with a large amount of cash.

Ability to have a spare cassette. Can load faster. You load a spare cassette at home or in your office and simply swap them at the location to load cash. Whenever the cassette that is in the machine is running out of cash, load the other one and simply replace the empty cassette with it.

They are an upgrade and typically part of higher-end ATMs.

Removable cassettes also come in a multi-cassette dispenser configuration, which holds 2 different currencies, twice as much cash for very busy locations or places where loading $10s and $20s or different denominations would increase profits.

Near-End Detection and Note shortage detection, which can help to reduce reversals or journal requests.

Cons

You have to learn how to remove the cassette. This requires opening up the ATM and extracting the cassette. There is more wear and tear when you remove and install the cassette all of the time, as well as a possible risk of damage.

Removable cassettes are generally an upgrade, which increases the price of the ATM.

Typical removable cassette specs:

CDU Type: Cassette (removable)

Maintenance: Front Service

Cassette Capacity: Max. 1000, 1700, and 2000 notes depending on the model (rated for new US notes). Typically holds less for recycled currency.

Reject Capacity: Reject Bin: Max. 200 notes

Dispense Speed: 3 Sheets/sec

Note Pick up: Friction Type

Power Supply: DC24V, 5V

Dimension: 270mm * 295mm * 430mm(W*H*D)

Weight: < 10kg

Near-End Detection: Yes

Note Shortage Detection: Yes

Which One Should You Use?

Comparing the two types of cassettes is a tricky prospect. Both of them have their pros and cons. Therefore, it comes down to deciding which cassette you should use or how busy the location is going to be. Keep in mind that the number of bills you can keep in the machine using either cassette is pretty much the same, so you don't have to stick to a particular type of cassette in this regard.

In terms of security, removable cassettes are better. Plus, you can get better support for them. Taking the important factors into account, it is hard to argue that removable cassettes aren't superior to fixed note cassettes. Fixed cassettes are fine for most installations, but if you are the type of person that wants the best, the deciding factor here is cost. If you can afford the upgrade costs or the ATM comes with a removable cassette, the choice is easy: go for a removable cassette. Otherwise, you have to stick with a fixed note cassette. If you are putting an ATM into a location that you are not sure will be very busy, save the upgrade costs and go with the fixed cassette. Sometimes, you can find sales or deals on ATM's with one or the other type of cassette. So, if a really good model ATM is on sale, just use whatever it comes with. Ask the ATM company you work with if they have specials or if they can notify you when they have deals.

Best Denominations to Use

An important consideration that not many ATM business owners pay attention to is the denominations of bills they use. As you know, there are different options for you to select from. You can go as low as $1 and as high as $100. So, which are the best denominations to use for ATMs?

There was a time when nearly every ATM in the US dispensed only $20 bills. Before that, you could get $5 and

$10, but $20 became standard. The reason for this is that it is cheaper and more efficient to stick to one denomination. There are different 'bins' (Cassettes) for each denomination, each one with a specific capacity. If you want to use different denominations, you need to install a dispenser that has multiple cassettes.

Therefore, it is much more convenient to stick to $20s. It can be said that $20s provides a fine balance between the highest and lowest possible withdrawals. That being said, serving odd numbers like $55 becomes difficult. However, most ATM users are accustomed to using the quick cash withdrawal features anyway.

When you initially set up your ATM and submit your paperwork (we'll discuss paperwork in another chapter), you'll have to tell the ATM service provider what denomination you will be loading. You can't easily switch as a preventative measure. If you accidentally load $10s into a machine that thinks its dispensing $20s, your customers will be shorted, and you will get complaint notices and automated reversals. Also, if you load $20s into a machine that is set up to dispense $10s, you'll be giving customers twice as much and won't usually have a way to recover unless you get an honest ATM user to call you. This is why we always recommend doing a transaction yourself and taking out at least the minimum amount every time you load the ATM. Completing a withdrawal on your own ATM will let you know it's working properly, help to prevent any mistakes, and avoid unnecessary trips back to the location. We have learned this from experience. Pay yourself the surcharge and do a withdrawal; it will save you in the long run.

There have been numerous studies about what denomination is the most profitable. While banks prefer you load $20s, as they are the most common denomination and easiest to obtain at the bank, loading some machines with $10s can be more profitable. And in some cases, just loading $5s can be great. If you have an ATM that is located near vending machines, a self-service car wash, or Laundromat, many of the machines in these facilities that accept bills only accept $5s or $10s, so be sure to check this if you plan to operate an ATM in these venues.

We've also seen that dispensing $10 bills in ATMs in less desirable neighborhoods with low-end liquor and convenience stores, for example, or stores in bad areas (bars on windows and doors) do better with $10s.

Individuals getting government benefits or low-income areas may not have large balances in their accounts. These individuals often just need $10 or don't have much more than that. By offering an ATM that services these individuals, you capture that niche in the marketplace.

Benefits of ATMs

We rarely think about having to run to the bank to get cash. Many of us take it for granted that, any time you are outdoors and run out of cash, you can simply visit the nearest ATM and withdraw the amount you need. You only need to have your ATM card, and you are good to go. This is a great option for people who don't like carrying too much cash. Plus, it offers a cushion in case you run out of cash while shopping or purchasing something expensive.

There is no doubt that people have become accustomed and dependent on ATMs, and it would be difficult for individuals to conduct commerce without them. But do ATMs benefit businesses as well?

In the beginning, I mentioned that you can make a steady income operating an ATM business. It is a lucrative industry and offers plenty of opportunities for success. However, this cannot be considered a benefit per se.

The issue is that most business owners don't have any idea how valuable having an ATM on the premises can prove to be. This is why some business owners don't entertain the notion of having one installed, or they are just too busy to take the time to understand the principles of ATM benefits. Similarly, there are numerous benefits of owning and operating an ATM business.

Benefits of ATMs for Retail Business Owners

Business owners in the retail sector can benefit from having an ATM machine in their stores. According to data collected, retail stores that have an ATM machine on location make more sales and prove to be more successful. The most significant reason for this is that people have to come in if they want to use the ATM. Since they are in the store and withdrawing cash, they often end up buying small items or impulse items.

In fact, notifying people that you have an ATM on your premises can increase the foot traffic in your store. More people coming in simply means you will have more customers. It is up to you to determine how you are going to convert the ATM users into your customers. Otherwise, it is pretty much a given that more people will enter your store once you hang a sign outside advertising you have an ATM in your store.

There is also the psychological factor to be considered. When people have money in their pockets, which they do after performing an ATM transaction, they might just buy something on impulse. There are few opportunities for businesses to trigger the impulse buying reaction people have. This way, store owners can get more people to shop without any marketing gimmicks.

You can be shrewd with the placement of your ATM. If you have it set up right next to the bargain counter, it is possible that you might be able to increase your sales substantially. A small retail business could generate hundreds of dollars in additional profits on a weekly basis simply by installing an ATM.

The biggest advantage is for businesses that operate on a cash basis. This goes for any retail business, small or large. More significantly, customers prefer to pay with cash more often than use credit cards, hence lowering credit card processing fees. Since customers can withdraw cash at the store, merchants benefit by avoiding the credit card fee. Plus, customers don't have to accumulate debt every time they go shopping.

Of course, you cannot overlook the fact that ATM customers might be looking to break a large bill. To do that, they would be forced to buy from you. Large retail stores might not be too impressed by this, but installing an ATM could make a huge difference to the profitability of a small business. In any case, you are receiving a fee when people use your ATM, even if they don't buy anything. It is a win-win situation for everyone.

All in all, installing an ATM at a business location is a great opportunity for the business owner. Not only are they likely to attract more customers, they also make money with the fees being charged to people for using the ATM.

Benefits of Owning and Operating an ATM Business

The income you generate from your ATM business is the foremost advantage. The fact that you have little to do to keep your machine(s) up and running makes it more of a passive income option than anything. The ATM company you work with will help you to set up the machine and program it. You don't have to be physically present at the location, unless of course the ATM is installed on your business premises.

The capital outlay for an ATM business is also limited. You only need to invest in the machines, which you can buy on credit if necessary. There are no major operating costs. The overhead is easily covered by the income from the transactions performed every day on your ATM. You can set up a full-fledged ATM business, installing five or six machines for under $25,000, which includes the cost of the equipment and enough to start loading cash. If you want to get a business equipment loan from a bank or line of credit for the equipment, then you only need cash for your inventory. The passive income from just 5 - 6 ATM's in an average location (5 - 6 transaction per day) would be between $1500 - $2500 per month (depending on your surcharge and any revenue split with the location owner). Obviously, the income from busy ATM locations is going to be much higher.

Even though there are close to 500,000 ATMs already operational across the US, there are still plenty of locations where there is demand and need for an ATM. So, there are perfectly viable opportunities for you to avail and set up your ATM business.

Last, but not least, it is highly unlikely that the demand for ATMs falls in the near future. More people have begun realizing the fact that withdrawing cash and performing transactions on ATMs is safe and reliable. Therefore, the demand is on the rise. So, you can expect a steady number of transactions per day with the right locations. With time, you will realize the scope of your business and decide whether or not you want to expand.

These are several benefits of owning and operating an ATM business. As you can see, it is a great business idea and has been since 1994. It continues to generate passive income for IADs nationwide. The only potential drawback of starting an ATM business is that you may install ATM machines in lower transaction locations, which would still turn an annualized percentage that far exceeds keeping money in a local bank account or CD. Even if you install an ATM in a location that only produces 40 -60 transactions monthly (that's just 2 - 3 transactions per day) at a $2.50 surcharge you could still earn upwards of 25% - 40% return on your investment, and that's if the ATM is in a bad location.

If this is a risk you are willing to take, this business is for you. If you follow the tips and advice provided to you in this book, you shouldn't have any trouble in making your ATM business a profitable venture for you.

Training and Operation

Using an ATM machine to perform a transaction as a customer and operating it as the owner are obviously two different things. There are several functions you have to master before you can run an ATM machine as a successful business.

Learning the Functions

While it is easier to load an ATM machine than a cash register and even a napkin holder, proper training and experience can help to avoid costly mistakes.

Even if you are not the one who is going to be physically operating the machine and loading the cash, it is imperative that you understand how the process works. For one, you may have to train someone else to do the job for you eventually. Secondly, in case the other person is unavailable, you may have to operate the machine anyway. This is why it's important to learn the different functions of the various ATM machines you own.

The great thing about modern ATMs is that they are fully-functional and programmed in a way that makes it convenient for the owner to operate them. You will receive an owner's manual with each machine you purchase. However, even if you consult the manual, it is quite possible that you might need a more in-depth understanding at times. So, what do you do in that situation?

Where Can You Get Training for Operating your ATM?

Your best option is to get professional training for operating the ATM. Having someone teach you how to work the machine is better than reading about it and then trying it. This is not to say that it can't be done, but getting professional experience is always better than trial and error. This is why it is important that you take some time and receive proper training.

The great thing about this business is that most ATM providers offer training services. When you place an order for an ATM, ask if they provide training. If yes, ask them how the training takes place. Do you need to travel to a special office, does someone come to you during installation, can it be done over the phone, online, etc.? There are many options. I prefer to have training done at the time of the first ATM installation. This is the ideal situation. This way, you will be completely adept and familiar with the workings of the ATM machine you own. You can virtually guarantee there is no downtime for your machines if you are properly trained in handling any issues.

The best ATM providers don't charge extra for training if done during the installation process. While the machine is being installed and programmed to bring it into working condition, you should be taught the various functions of the machine. The installer will cover every aspect of the machine that you need to know in order to operate it successfully.

In order to make the most of your ATM business, it is imperative that your machines are up and running all of the time. For that, you need to understand what to check and when, as well as any necessary actions that are required if there is an issue. That is only possible if you know how to do it. So, get in touch with your ATM provider and discuss the training process.

Revenues

This is perhaps the most relevant of all topics covered in this book. The purpose of setting up an ATM business is for you to build wealth, earn a nice passive income, work fewer hours than a full-time job, and get a much higher annual return from cash than money that is just sitting in a bank account.

When it comes to revenue from your ATM business, it will most likely be in the form of fees. The customers who use your machine will be charged a fee for each transaction they perform using your machine. The more transactions you can generate and the more customers you can attract, the greater your revenue will be. This is known as the surcharge fee.

What is a Surcharge Fee?

You will hear many people pose the question: "Why do I have to pay a surcharge to access my own cash from the ATM?" The answer to that is quite simple. Customers have a choice. They can make a trip to their own bank to get money from a teller, or they can locate one of their own bank's ATMs. While these are great choices for consumers, people are busy, find they are short on cash, and it's inconvenient to locate an ATM from their bank.

Your ATM machine offers consumers a convenient option. For this convenience, they are charged a fee. This is especially the case since you have to invest in the equipment and keep it loaded with cash. In reality, an ATM is simply a Cash Dispensing Vending Machine. The only product is cash. It's the same principle as the additional cost to get sodas or snacks from machines. It's convenient, and someone has to own and load the machines.

While banks do not usually charge a surcharge fee on their ATMs for their own customers, non-banking customers will typically be charged. Some virtual banks without ATMs also reimburse surcharge fees to their customers.

The Amazing Money Machine

You are going to be a private ATM owner, and one of the ways you will make money is through the surcharge fee. You can set the fee according to your preference. Typically, the range in which the surcharge fee generally falls is $1.00 to $8.00. Fees vary due to many factors. The average fee nationwide is about $2.50; however, some large financial institutions are now charging $3.00 to non-bank customers. To determine the best surcharge for your machine, visit the competition in the area where you plan to install the machine and speak with your ATM company representative until you are comfortable and have the experience to maximize that revenue.

Keep in mind the fact that there are a few other costs associated with owning and operating an ATM. Your costs are going to include the machine, which will cost between $2,000 - $5,000 or more depending on the model and features needed. Other costs include maintenance, service, receipt paper, communications, loading and reloading costs (gas and travel time), etc. While there are electricity costs, these are typically minimal and paid by the location owner. You have to cover the costs in some way, and charging a surcharge fee is the best way to do so.

You can increase or decrease the surcharge fee with your ATM provider; however, there could be fees associated with that process. You'll soon figure out the best fee for each machine to maximize your revenue.

What is Interchange?

Also known as an interbank fee, interchange is the fee banks have to pay the networks like Plus, Cirrus, Star, NYCE, etc. for routing the transactions to the appropriate account for out-of-network transactions. When you use your own bank's ATM machine, they know your account information and usually do not have to route your ATM transaction through a 3rd-party network. These transactions stay in-house (aka in-network) and usually do not require the bank to pay any interchange.

Interchange is only paid on out-of-network transactions. Since your ATM will always be out of the customer's network, the customer's bank will have to pay the interchange, so customers will often get charged a bank fee for using an out-of-network ATM in addition to the surcharge. (Some online banks like E*Trade, Discover and Bank of Internet may reimburse some or all of these fees to their customers.) Usually, local, regional, and some national banks charge customers to encourage them to use in-network ATMs so they can avoid the fees.

However, when bank customers have to perform ATM transactions urgently or for convenience reasons and select an ATM other than their own bank, the only option for that ATM is to perform an out-of-network transaction. In that case, the customer may also be charged an out-of-network fee by their bank that most likely then pays various network fees.

This means that the customer's bank is paying the network and the ATM processing company for enabling him or her to perform the withdrawal or any other transaction on out-of-network ATMs. In many cases, ATM companies do not divulge the details regarding the interchange being paid by the bank. If you have a large portfolio of ATMs or are building your ATM business and do not participate in the interchange, it could mean you are losing out on a substantial chunk of additional revenue.

Keep in mind that everyone supporting your ATM business needs to keep the doors open and to pay their employees so they answer the phones when you call for help or need support with your business. A good ATM provider will be transparent about fees and revenue and will disclose everything upfront. Unfortunately, some ATM providers, like many industries, are opportunists instead of partners. These types of companies may try to hide the interchange, charge you erroneous fees, and not really care if your ATM business makes money or not.

Before surcharging, the interchange was the only way banks were compensated for letting non-account holders use their ATMs. Also keep in mind that commercial ATMs that banks install can cost ten to twenty times more than the ATMs we deploy.

Each network has different interchange rates, structures, and tiers. Interchange is constantly changing and is typically how the ATM processing companies, bank sponsors, and other entities involved in the business get paid.

Some ATM companies will share some of the interchange with IADs, depending on the volume of transactions. Some ATM companies also offer pass-through pricing, also known as flat rate, buy rate, or net rate pricing. This is where they pass on the entire surcharge and the interchange to the IAD and then simply charge the IAD one flat fee for each transaction. If you build up your ATM business to where you are processing thousands or tens of thousands of ATM transactions, be sure the ATM company you work with will offer you pass-through pricing once you learn the business, have enough transactions, and take on additional responsibilities to warrant that rate structure.

Again, this comes down to the provider you select. You should ensure that the ATM provider you select is reliable and reputable (and has been in the business a long time so your residuals are never at risk). Then you can rest assured that some of the interchange fees generated through your machine will be paid to you. This is one way to maximize revenues from your ATM business.

What are Acquirer Fees?

There are a lot of terms used in this business when you first start that can be confusing. Don't get bogged down in all of the different terms. Just know that you earn revenue from Surcharges and Interchange (if you participate), and there could be some fees known as acquirer fees. These fees are charged on a small portion of the transactions (depending on the cards used in your ATM). The acquirer fees are small charges that vary from 1 cent to 18 cents as of this writing and are from a variety of different networks.

1. MasterCard imposes its service and other fees against the Interchange and pays the difference to the ATM acquirer of the transaction. Beginning April 1, 2010, MasterCard implemented a tiered system that now charges its card-issuing banks different amounts based on transaction volume.

2. MasterCard imposes its fees against these tiered amounts. This means the net interchange paid by MasterCard is as low as $0.17 per ATM transaction, depending on the transaction volume of the card-issuing bank.

3. MasterCard's April 16, 2010 Pricing Change affected each ATM withdrawal involving a U.S.-issued card used at an ATM located in the U.S. MasterCard now charges both a $0.05 Program Support Fee on each ATM withdrawal and a variable Brand Volume Fee of 0.095% of the amount withdrawn to the ATM acquirer. Both of these fees are subtracted from the net interchange. Beginning April 16, 2010, the Program Support Fee increased from $0.05 to $0.18

for each withdrawal, and the Brand Volume Fee was eliminated. The result is that lower-volume ATM Deployers are often seeing this $0.18 fee coming out of their revenue. Visa followed suit and also added a similar Acquirer fee to Visa Surcharged Transactions, as did several other networks, including Pulse, NYCE, and a few others. Acquirer fees currently range from $0.01 - $0.18. Some ATM Companies charge a flat acquirer fee to eliminate accounting and statement nightmares between reporting networks.

4. Pulse, a subsidiary of Discover Financial Services Company, also announced a pricing change effective May 1, 2010. For all U.S. approved and declined ATM cash withdrawals and cash advances, Pulse will charge a new fee, called the U.S. ATM Acquirer Fee, in the amount of $0.03. This new U.S. ATM Acquirer Fee is in addition to Pulse's existing ATM Network Security Fee of $0.01, applied to all U.S. and International approved and declined ATM cash withdrawals and cash advances.

Keep in mind that the fees are by network, so if you're working with an ATM provider that offers priority routing, connecting your ATMs to local regional networks whenever possible, your fees will vary. It's all based on the ATM cards inserted by your customers and the routing from your ATM provider. ATMDepot uses priority routing and tries to avoid fees or keep them to a minimum whenever possible. Keep in mind that these fees involving pennies per transaction only occur on surcharge transactions. So, the fee you charge easily offsets any network fee.

So, those are the three types of fees you need to know about when projecting the revenue for your ATM business. The customers have to pay you for using your machine without any doubt. The surcharge is where the bulk of your income will be derived. If you receive any interchange income, it is often used to offset the acquirer fees. Depending on the network usage, these fees can reduce your monthly revenue, but only slightly. As long as you are getting some portion of the interchange fee, the acquirer fees can be a wash and not reduce your monthly revenue at all.

Bank Networks

As highlighted in the beginning of the book, your ATMs will be connected to a processing provider that will connect your ATM with the proper networks to be operational. There is no way you can get your machines up and running if they aren't connected to a network. First, you need to understand what interbank networks are.

What Are Interbank Networks?

It wouldn't be wrong to say that most people take ATMs for granted now. Many people no longer withdraw cash by making a trip to the bank. They find the nearest ATM and perform all of their transactions there or online. What is amazing about ATM technology is that customers can withdraw money from a machine even if it isn't owned and operated by their bank.

This is where interbank networks are at work. The interbank networks allow people to withdraw cash from any machine on the network regardless of the bank they keep their money in. The interbank network is what allows the customer to perform the transactions they do on ATM machines. The interesting thing is that few, if any, users actually know what goes into performing an ATM transaction.

There are several interbank networks in operation currently, including Plus, Cirrus, PULSE, AFFN and STAR, along with a host of other networks. When a customer performs a transaction on the machine, the relevant information is relayed by the machine to the customer's bank. The information is then used to attribute the transaction to the customer's account.

The machines themselves are connected through a Controller. Nowadays, most retail ATM machines utilize a high-speed internet connection or a wireless device. This ensures that their customers get to enjoy speedy service and keep coming back to use the machine.

Customers can still perform out-of-network transactions on the ATMs near them. However, sometimes, the fee charged is higher than that on an in-network ATM. This is why most people prefer to withdraw cash from an ATM machine operated by their bank.

There are two main types of interbank networks: regional and national.

How Regional Networks Differ from National Networks?

As an ATM business owner, you should know the difference between the two types of networks so you can ask the right questions when selecting an ATM provider.

Regional networks are typically on ATM cards from regional banks, but can also be utilized by national banks, though less often.

Regional networks include Star and NYCE, for example, while national networks include Plus (owned by Visa) and Cirrus (owned by MasterCard).

Customers banking with a regional bank may see the logo of a regional network on the back of their ATM cards, while customers of National Banks will often see the logos of National Networks.

National networks, as their name implies, span the entire country, while regional networks are obviously located in specific areas of the U.S.

If you bank with a small community bank that only offers regional network access and you travel to an area of the country or internationally, you may not be able to find an ATM that offers that network. However, most ATM providers now offer all-network access. The key is to find an ATM provider that not only offers access to the most networks, but also offers smart or priority transaction routing to the most profitable network available for each ATM Card presented.

The Process

The process is where you get to learn about how the withdrawals are made and how you get your money back. In terms of running an ATM business, this is an important chapter. Though it may not be as comprehensive or exhaustive as the other topics, there is little doubt that one needs to understand the process completely.

How Long Does It Take for the Money To Get Back Into My Account?

A question people unfamiliar with the ATM business commonly ask is where the cash in the machine comes from. The answer to that is quite simple: from the cash vaulter's account. If you are the owner of the ATM machine, you have to decide who will be loading the cash. This person is the vaulter. If you decide to put your own money into the machine, you would be the ATM owner, operator, and vaulter, which of course is the best way to make the most money.

As the owner, it is your responsibility to ensure that the machine does not run out of cash. If you have delegated the vaulting duties to a 3rd-party or vaulting service provider, those responsibilities would transfer to them. Most ATM companies offer some type of vaulting service.

After a few months, you will have a clear idea of the peak hours and prime days during which the withdrawals would be busier than usual. If you are doing the cash loading yourself, you can use your ATM company's online system to keep track of the cash balance in the ATM to help you manage the replenishment cycle so the machine does not run out of cash, and you can also ensure you are not loading more cash than necessary.

So, if you are putting your cash into the machine and people are withdrawing it, how do you get it back? The ATM company you work with or their 3rd-party provider will move the money into your account via ACH (Automated Clearing House) via the Federal Reserve

Banking System. You will receive a deposit for each day's ATM transactions on the following business banking day.

The cut off time for the ATMDepot.com ATM service is from 1pm to 12:59pm PT. For example, if someone uses my ATMs here in California between Monday 1pm and Tuesday at 12:59 pm, all the funds withdrawn between those times are put back in my bank account on Wednesday morning. The ACH happens the previous day overnight, so your bank credits your account the next morning. In the example above, the funds move through the Federal Reserve Tuesday evening and are then credited to my settlement account Wednesday morning.

Since the weekends and holidays are not banking days, funds withdrawn from Friday at 1pm to Sunday at 12:59pm are deposited Monday (three separate deposits, one for each day). If Friday or Monday happens to be a holiday, it pushes the deposit to Tuesday.

If you are not working with ATMDepot.com, make sure you ask the ATM company you select to tell you their daily cash settlement policy so you know the exact schedule when funds are put back into your account.

Cash settlement timing varies among ATM providers; be sure you understand the schedule, as it can affect your business' cash flow significantly. Selecting a good service would mean that if the cash was withdrawn on Monday, it would be back in your account on Tuesday as in my example above. So, for example, if you are in New York and work with ATMDepot.com, all funds withdrawn prior to 4:00pm ET would be deposited back into the settlement account on Tuesday.

There are some ATM providers that delay settlement to use the float, since most are moving millions of dollars, and one extra day delay can make a big difference to them as well as you. If you have a lot of ATMs and you are the vaulter, you want the fastest settlement possible.

What's the Process for Withdrawal?

Using an ATM has become one of the most convenient means of taking out cash from a bank account. This is why people prefer using the machines instead of making a trip to the bank. The process for withdrawal is quite simple, which is one of the major reasons why ATM machines are so popular. The customer simply has to insert his/her debit or credit card (depending on the machine) into the dip or swipe reader on the machine.

The machine then prompts the person to enter his/her PIN code and, from there on in, the instructions for making a withdrawal are displayed on the screen. The person making the withdrawal doesn't have to think too hard about what to do. The process is uniform for virtually all ATM machines.

Working with Your Bank

Choosing the Right Bank

There are lots of banks out there to choose from, and the right banking relationship can save you time and money. I recommend starting with a bank you already have a relationship with.

The easiest way to manage your ATM deposits is by opening a separate bank account for your ATM business. The processor will automatically make deposits into your bank account daily so, while there won't be a lot of transactional volume going through your account (3 deposits on Monday, then 1 deposit each other business day, up to 30 or so deposits monthly), some banks may think this is more than average.

It's time consuming to manage your personal and business transactions in one account, so to make it easier, I suggest a separate bank account for each ATM you operate. This can help you to keep track and account for all of the cash you allocate to each machine. While some IADs prefer to use one account, I prefer one for each machine, but everyone has his/her preferences. You can always start with one and, if it gets confusing or you don't like all of your funds for all of your ATMs in the same account, open more accounts and then let your ATM provider know you need to submit account changes. It's only one form, but may take a few days for the settlement funds to catch up to the changes.

Let the bank know there will only be 30 total deposits into your account each month because, sometimes, they will have different fee structures for various types of transaction volume. Each time your ATM is low on cash, you will need to visit the bank and withdraw the funds from your account to reload the ATM. This could bring your account to a zero balance if you are using all of the available funds to reload cash.

When opening a new account with the bank, let them know that you will need an account that has no monthly fees (or lowest possible fees; many banks offer accounts that cost less than $10.00 per month). It's also a good idea to mention that the balance could reach zero dollars.

Keep in mind that all banks operate differently and have different criteria. For example, your bank may have a minimum balance requirement of $100.00, and therefore you will need to maintain a $100.00 balance in order to avoid the monthly fees. The simple solution would be to keep an extra $100.00 in your account at all times to avoid any fees.

Therefore, if you have $1000.00 in your account for reloading cash, you will not want to withdraw more than $900.00, leaving you with a balance of $100.00 to avoid a monthly bank fee. Other banks may ask you to set up a savings account to link to your business account with an automatic monthly transfer of $100.00 from checking to savings. This is another easy way to avoid paying fees. You can easily transfer the money back to your checking account a few days after the automatic transfer.

Whatever bank you select, just make sure you account for any fees and keep a ledger so you always balance your cash monthly.

Cash Needs

It's a good idea to introduce yourself to the Merchant Teller as well as the branch manager at your bank. You want to make sure they are aware of your business and cash needs. A good starting amount is $2,000 - $3,000 each week per machine.

The Merchant Teller is usually in charge of ordering Cash for the branch, and will want to make sure they can accommodate your needs. The bank will usually stock plenty of $20s, but may need to special-order $10s in case you need them. If you add more machines down the road, you will need to increase your cash order with the bank as needed.

Here are some suggestions that make it easier for the bank to work with you. Following these suggestions can make you more attractive to work with, make the process more efficient, and can save you money in fees.

Pick up your cash on a set day every week. Sometimes, the armored carriers that bring cash to the banks make deposits on a certain day of the week. If you can pick up on that same day, the bank will pay less in interest.

Call Ahead – Give the merchant teller ample time to have your cash ready. This will save you time waiting at the branch and will help to keep the lines moving.

Withdrawal Slip – Fill it out in advance for each account. Be sure to include all of your account information and cash totals.

Be prepared and professional.

Be sure to appreciate the job they do for you. Bringing the Merchant Teller a gift during the holidays and something on his/her birthday if you end up finding out when that is goes a long way in relationship building.

If you are just starting off and loading $20s into only one ATM, cash loading is simple. You can even pull all of your cash loading funds directly from the ATM at your bank. Sometimes, your bank will allow you to increase the maximum withdrawal amount on your debit card to $1,000.00, giving you the capability of withdrawing all your money from the ATM if you don't require more than $1,000.00.

You need special permission from the bank to have a limit this high, but considering your line of business, it should be approved. This will help you to save time and have access to cash even when the banks are closed on Sundays. Keep in mind that having a high limit is a convenience, but is also a security risk as well. If your bank card and pin number are stolen, it would be easier for the thief to get more cash from your account. This is a very rare occurrence, but worth mentioning.

Cash Loading Safety Tips

Try to load cash on alternate days and times.

Try to load cash during daylight hours.

Keep cash in your pocket or in an unmarked bag.

Try to maintain a low profile.

When opening the safe with the combination, try to cover the numbers with your free hand and always assume you are being watched.

Ordering an ATM Machine

Now that you have some idea of the paperwork and documentation involved in placing an order for an ATM machine, now is the time to learn how to actually place the order.

How Do I Order An ATM?

You can place the order for an ATM machine with a reputable ATM provider. The providers are well-versed about the paperwork and other formalities necessary to complete your order. There are some things you will have to figure out before you place the order. Are you going to buy the machine out right (check or credit card), are you going to lease, get a loan, or ask about creative financing? Some providers accept credit cards for the machine, while others don't. Some providers will even accept payments over a short term if you are processing transactions with them. Some providers will offer low-cost leasing as well as loans (loans are typically for $10K and up, so if you plan to purchase 4 – 6 machines, a loan is worth looking into).

Furthermore, you have to decide whether you want to buy a new machine or a refurbished one (if any are available); in either case, talk to your ATM provider. They can help you to select the best machine for the location, will ensure that the order is placed correctly, and that the machine is delivered to you in the shortest time possible.

In summary, if you're not working with ATMDepot.com, find a reliable ATM provider and get the ATM machine you want. It's as simple as completing an equipment order form. See the link index for further information.

Where Does It Ship From and To?

As far as new machines are concerned, they are usually shipped directly from the manufacturer's location. This guarantees that the machine you are purchasing has a recent manufacturer's date (which you can verify on a decal inside of the top of the ATM), is current with all of the updated ADA requirements, and has all of the necessary and current network security requirements as well.

In the case of refurbished ATMs, sometimes, the processing partner or your ATM provider may ship the machine. The reason for this is that the machine has to be cleaned, tested, and programmed for installation. You also want to make sure it is still a model that can process transactions on the networks (if you get a refurbished ATM from anywhere else, there is no guarantee it will work with your provider).

In either case, the address you provide on the equipment order form should be where you want the ATM shipped. Unless you have an easy method to transport the ATM, it's always best to ship the machine to where it's going to be installed.

Paperwork & Documentation

Once you have made the decision to set up an ATM business, it is time you order a machine. Before you can do so, there are a few things you need to figure out. First of all, you need to have a clear idea of the number of ATM machines you want to set up. Most new ATM entrepreneurs start with one machine to get their feet wet. Speak with your ATM provider to get the latest info on the best machines for your proposed location or to see if there are any specials, sales, or incentives for one machine over another.

Next, you'll have to complete the necessary paperwork for purchasing the ATM and the documents for ATM processing, or you won't be able to operate it. This would mean that you would have an ATM machine delivered without the documentation to program it or operate it. This is especially true if you purchase an ATM from a company that does not also provide processing or if you purchased a used ATM machine from a classified ad or online auction site. Be careful purchasing used machines. Many of them are out of compliance and, what appears to be a good deal, is really an expensive boat anchor.

For someone new to the ATM business, the paperwork can be a potential stumbling block. In fact, some people even get discouraged to the extent that they reconsider their decision to start an ATM business. However, the process itself is not that difficult. You only need to keep a few things in mind, and you shouldn't face any problems at all.

The main concern is unfamiliarity. If you know about the paperwork and documentation required, you wouldn't be as surprised and overwhelmed as some people get. Keeping this in mind, here is a general overview of the paperwork required for ordering and setting up an ATM.

Paperwork for Ordering an ATM

There are a series of forms and contracts that you need to complete and sign before you can order the machine and have it up and running. There are various reasons why completing the necessary paperwork is important:

You need to prove your credentials and identity. For setting up an ATM business, or any business for that matter, you need to provide the relevant documentation and your ID. This way, the underwriters (similar to getting a bank account) can verify your identity and perform the required background checks.

Running an ATM machine means you are conducting money wire transactions for other people. As per the law of the land, a criminal or felon is not allowed to operate such a business. Completing the paperwork ensures that your sponsoring bank and processing center complete the proper due diligence so as to comply with all legalities and know clearly that you are not a felon and are allowed to run an ATM business. If you are unsure, ask your ATM provider.

Certain parts of the paperwork processing include government requirements for compliance purposes in order to own and operate an ATM machine. Try as you may, you cannot get around the requirements imposed by the Federal Government. If you don't complete and submit the necessary paperwork, you won't be able to get your business operational.

You can get in touch with your ATM provider about the forms that you have to complete and submit when ordering the machine. They will guide you in the right direction, virtually guaranteeing that you can set up your business in a legal manner. Rather than trying on your own to get the paperwork done, you should seek professional help. This will ensure that you get the process completed quickly.

There is one thing you do need to keep in mind when ordering an ATM. You have to decide on the service fee you are going to charge your customers and the currency denominations you are going to load into your machines before you submit the paperwork. Therefore, it is crucial that you decide on these two things before you order the machine. You might have to do some research to make an informed decision.

Paperwork for Setting up an ATM

Part of the paperwork includes the Equipment Order Form. Once you have completed this form and ordered the ATM, you have to prepare to get it set up. You don't have to do much in the way of the actual installation process. The company you order the machine from will deliver, install and program the machine as per your instructions. Some ATM providers will help train you to program the ATM yourself, saving you some of the programming fee. What you do have to do is to complete and submit the relevant paperwork for setting up the machine.

There are numerous things you have to consider. These include:

1. Deciding what the Surcharge fee is going to be.

2. Deciding the denominations you want the ATM to dispense (usually $20s).

3. What bank and bank account you are going to link the ATM to. Without having a bank you can work with, you cannot run an ATM business. This is why you should figure this out beforehand, as some banks can take from a few days to a few weeks to set up an account for the ATM business. You will need a voided check or a bank letter. We have found that speaking to your bank about your new ATM business before you start is best. Some banks have

strict policies about working companies that require a lot of cash. Be certain you are forthcoming with your bank to avoid any speed bumps in the road to success.

4. Are you going to install the ATM yourself or have a professional do it for you?

As far as setting up the ATM is concerned, you need to ensure that the location you selected is ready and that you have obtained the proper SLA placement agreement with the location owner prior to the time the machine is delivered.

Complete the required processing paperwork at the same time you order the machine, if possible. It's okay to have the machine delivered first if you want to get familiar with it yourself and get trained on how to program it. If the location where you are placing the ATM is nearby, you can have the ATM delivered to your home instead of the location, but be sure you have a vehicle big enough so that you can deliver it when it comes time to install it.

Are There Contracts?

Of course, where there are documents to complete, there are going to be a few contracts. First and foremost, you have to complete a purchase agreement with the company you are going to buy the machines from. Your ATM provider is your sole source of support and guidance; therefore, you cannot be successful without speaking and working with one. Of course, I recommend ATMDepot.com, but feel free to call around and find someone you are comfortable working with.

You will have to work with a local bank (one that you already do business with is a good start). Make an appointment with the branch manager and let them know you'll be starting an ATM business. They can walk you through opening the accounts. We recommend opening one checking account for each machine, but that is not a requirement. I use one account for each machine so it's easier on the accounting. Some of our IADs use one account for all of the machines and simply download the deposits and track them in QuickBooks.

Lastly, you need to decide whether or not you're going to be loading the ATM machine, if you're going to hire someone to do it for you, or if the location manager or location owner is going to load the ATM. What this means is that each different function and operation related to your ATM business requires you to have some sort of agreement.

If you're going to contract with a third-party provider to load the ATM, this may require an additional contract unless, of course, you intend to perform that function yourself, which most new ATM business people do.

These are some of the contracts, documents and forms you will need to complete to order and set up your ATM machines. Keep these in mind so that you can breeze through them and start running your business soon.

You should not be put off by the paperwork. There are not that many agreements when you work with certain companies. Here's a quick summary of the required documentation:

1. Equipment Order Form, usually completed by the ATM Provider.

2. ATM Application includes location information, personal information, and information required for a

background check. This is not a contract, but is a required document.

3. ATM Processing Agreement – lists obligations, responsibilities, terms and conditions of each party; this is a required legal document.

4. ACH – this is an Automated Clearing House document that authorizes the processor to make deposits to your bank account for daily settlement of funds, as well as your monthly commissions. It also authorizes them to debit your account for any adjustments, discrepancies, or errors (albeit rare).

5. You'll also need a Voided Business Check for the ACH. If your account is new or you don't have checks, you can request a bank letter on letterhead stating you have an account in good standing from your banker.

6. Lastly, you will need a clear, legible copy of your driver's license.

Optional, but recommended:

1. If you are placing the ATM in a 3rd-party location, you may want to protect yourself with a Placement Agreement. Again, if you work with ATMDepot.com you can find samples in the members' area of the website.

2. ATM Insurance: If you wish to purchase separate ATM insurance for each machine, a simple agreement with the provider is required. Insurance policies at the time of this writing start at just $12 per month.

Optional Hardware

When it comes to optional hardware you can buy for your ATM machines, a topper, an e-lock, and a wireless device are the foremost among them.

What is a Topper?

A topper is a type of screen or light that is installed on the ATM machine that either displays video or is just a translucent back lit panel with the letters ATM. Alternately, you can go to a sign shop or make arrangements with your ATM provider to get custom inserts for the toppers with your logo and phone number if you'd like, but really, it's meant to draw people to the ATM. Toppers are also a way you can use your machines for marketing. The sign and/or video on the topper can be used for many things. There was a time when ATM business owners had to think twice before investing in a topper. The equipment was expensive, and the concept of ATM-based marketing wasn't popular. Now, toppers pay for themselves.

With improvements in technology, the cost of purchasing an ATM topper has decreased significantly. This means that you can easily purchase a topper for your machines, sell advertising on them, or lease the space out to advertising companies if you have enough real estate. Also, people have begun to expect more from ATM machines. Installing a topper gives you the chance to capture their attention and also fulfill their expectations.

More than anything, you can use the topper screen to market your business. This is particularly helpful if you have installed your machine in a retail establishment. You will find it easier to retain customers and also attract more customers when you have a topper screen displaying such offers and rewards.

The technology used in ATM screens is now at the level where ATM businesses can make the most of topper screens. Therefore, when you decide to order an ATM machine, ask the provider if they offer topper screens as well. Toppers rarely come pre-installed. They typically ship separately and are an easy field install. If you hire or pay for professional installation, installing the topper is typically included. Otherwise, it's a very straightforward DIY job.

That being said, despite its various benefits, a video or illuminated topper (aka High Topper) remains a hardware option. They are fairly inexpensive, but some locations may not want them or have the space for them. If you plan to install a topper of any size as an optional component, be sure to get the measurements and plan appropriately. Be sure to note any height restrictions where you are installing the ATM. Also, be sure the location proprietor knows about the topper. The last thing you want is to go through the trouble of arranging a video topper and advertising only to have the location owner upset about it due to unmanaged expectations.

What is an E-Lock?

We covered locks earlier, but if you skipped ahead, an e-lock is an electronic lock for the safe portion of the ATM. Most ATMs come factory standard with a regular dial combination safe lock. You know the type. Three to the right, 2 to the left, 1 to the right until it stops. You get the idea. If you plan to load several machines at a time, or would like quick and easy access, upgrading to an e-lock is a no-brainer. You'll save hours of safe opening over the life of the machine. Costs are typically $50 – 100 for this upgrade at the time of ordering a new machine, depending on the type of ATM. If you wait to order it and want to do an elock upgrade in the field it's going to be a lot more expensive.

What is a Mas Hamilton Lock?

A Mas Hamilton (now Kaba-Mas or Cencon) lock is an upgraded lock required by most Armored Carriers. If you plan to have your ATM loaded by an armored carrier, this lock ensures that the opening and closing of the ATM is tracked for auditing. It requires special keys and computer software for the tracking of every entry. Each key is coded to the person opening the safe. The only reason to get this lock is if it's required by your vaulting vendor. Talk to your ATM company if you need this service for further details. These locks are a lot more expensive than any other lock.

What is a wireless device?

When setting up your machines, it is crucial that you ask the location if they have high speed Internet service so you can have them add a hardwired jack where you plan to place the ATM; otherwise, you should opt to purchase a wireless device from your ATM provider. These devices have a guarantee and are less expensive than the old phone lines and allow for unlimited transactions for a flat monthly fee. A wireless device will ensure your machine is operational at all times and that you have control over the communications functions. A wireless device uses secure encryption but sends the encrypted signal over cell phone networks. The data packets are so small and compressed with encryption that the monthly fee for unlimited transactions is typically less than the cost of the standard old phone lines. A wireless device ensures that your ATM is always available to communicate with the host and avoids most potential communication problems with phone lines. At the time of this writing, wireless device costs are between $7.99 - $19.99 per month, based on the wireless device hardware (which can be leased or purchased).

What other optional hardware is available?

There are a few other pieces of hardware that are not currently standard on ATMs as of this writing that you should be aware of.

EMV Card Reader upgrade:

EMV chip card transactions improve security against fraud compared to magnetic stripe card transactions. Currently, as of this writing, EMV card readers are optional. You can upgrade from the factory today for a fraction of what it will cost to get a field-upgraded EMV reader by the time it's required. I recommend this upgrade, but if you're on a tight budget, you can forgo it today, but keep in mind this is something you'll want to have before October 2016 for MasterCard and October 2017 for Visa transactions. After that, if your ATMs do not have EMV and there is fraud that could have been prevented by EMV, the liability shifts (transfers) from the ATM processing center to the ATM owner. There will be a huge opportunity to upgrade old equipment over the next few years.

Removable Cassette or Multiple Cassette Upgrade:

We spoke about cassettes in several other chapters; however, it's noteworthy to repeat it here since it is an optional hardware upgrade. Several ATM machines come standard with a fixed note cassette. This means that you have to fill the ATM in place. You can't remove the cassette and take it into the back room to fill it. If you plan to load a large amount of cash, load cash during open hours, or would like privacy during the loading of the cash, I highly recommend you opt for a removal cassette or get an ATM that comes with one standard.

Multiple-cassette ATMs are best suited for high traffic locations or locations where more than one denomination is required. In multiple-cassette ATMs, you can load as many denominations as there are cassettes. In a 2-cassette ATM you can load $10s and $20s if you like, for example, or if it's a busy casino, you may want to load $20s and $100's. Just be sure you load the right cassettes with the right denomination.

Surrounds and Wraps:

These are not really hardware options, but options nevertheless. These are decorative options and can be handy to help you win out over your competition. Surrounds are often required by hotels, and you can purchase nice standard or custom wooden surrounds. Many standard surrounds are available for most ATM models, but most cabinet shops can make a custom surround if necessary.

Wraps are typically graphics attached to the ATM. There are several brands. Have you ever seen a car, truck, bus or other vehicle with complete graphics wrapped around the entire body? Well, you can do the same thing to an ATM machine. Make your ATM look like anything you want with a custom graphic wrap. Pricing varies if you need it designed, but it's still very reasonable. Ask your ATM company what's available if you are interested in making your ATM stand out.

Cash

Most privately-owned ATMs are simply cash vending machines. Customers can only perform a few functions through these ATMs, which include cash transactions, balance inquiries, and transfers.

How Much Cash Does the Machine Hold?

While we have gone over the amount of cash your machine will hold, it's also worth repeating. It depends on the cassette you select. Cassettes vary in size from 800 notes to 2,000 notes. The two most common cassettes hold 700 or 1500 used notes. Of course, that is the maximum number of bills you can load. We recommend you start with $2000 - $3000 and monitor your ATM usage so you can best determine the right amount of cash needed. Once you have a better idea of the number of transactions performed on your machine, you'll be able to maximize your cash loading.

How Frequently Do You Need to Put Cash in the Machine?

As the owner of the business, it is up to you to decide the time at which you would reload the machine. However, rather than making this complicated, you can simply log into your online ATM dashboard and review your ATM balance or, as stated previously, setup text/SMS alerts. When your ATM begins to get low on cash, you will want to plan to load it soon. You can also set up a schedule once you know the busy days. For example, if the ATM is busy on weekends, you would want to be sure there are sufficient funds before Friday.

Again, the volume of transactions your machine is attracting will play a major role in determining how frequently you need to put cash into it. It is possible that you don't put more than 50 $20 bills in the machine at first. It might suffice, but the situation will change if the number of customers increases. In that case, you will have to load more cash or increase the frequency of putting cash into the machine.

What is the Maximum Surcharge?

Most states in the US don't have any legal limit for the surcharge fee you can impose on each transaction that is performed on your machine. Yet, that doesn't mean you can charge any amount you wish. For instance, if the average withdrawal transaction is $60, you would not want to charge $10. That would mean a substantial percentage of the withdrawn amount has to be spent by the customer for the withdrawal. There is a point of diminishing returns.

The surcharge fee is one thing that can actually drive people away if it is too high. This is why it is important that the surcharge fee you set for your machines is competitive, but not too low.

So, what is the maximum surcharge you can impose? The maximum surcharge depends not on any legal limit. Some states have restrictions. Rather than list all of the states here, you simply have to research about the surcharge fees being charged in your vicinity and then decide accordingly. Also, you need to keep in mind the location of your ATM. For instance, ATMs located in retail stores cannot charge a surcharge fee as high as those in a casino or other typical higher surcharge venues.

Here are some guidelines on how you can set the surcharge:

$2.00 to $2.75 – Fast Food Restaurants, Convenience Stores, Retailers, Barber Shop, Nail Salon

$2.50 to $3.95 – Nightclubs, Bars, Brewery

$4.00 and over – Casinos, Adult Entertainment

These are just general numbers based on observation from what ATMs located in these types of businesses usually charge their customers. Based on our experience, the ideal range for setting a surcharge fee to get the customers rolling in is $1.75 to $2.50. We have several machines charging just $1.00, some have no surcharge, and some charging $3.95 or more. It all depends on the location. In this regard, we would recommend you speak with your ATM provider to determine not just the maximum surcharge for a new location, but the best surcharge. Personally, I think it's best to start lower and slowly increase it once the machine gets busy.

How is the Passive Income Paid?

Many ATM Providers have different dates when they pay the residual commissions. This is the surcharge and any interchange portion of your revenue and is different than your settlement funds (money you load the ATM with).

Some ATM providers will pay the surcharge daily; however, I personally think this creates an accounting headache and adds double the number of deposits to your account that you need to track.

At ATM Depot, we prefer to receive residual commissions once a month, and we do the same for all of our ATM Business Partners. We will not only pay you, but we'll make sure you and anyone else you instruct us to pay (on the ACH forms) will receive all residual commissions by the 10th of each month following the month the transactions take place.

For example: If you instruct ATM Depot on your documents package that your ATM will surcharge $2.50 and you want us to pay your location $1.00 after the first 50 transactions, we can do that. So starting on the 51st transaction each month, they will get $1.00 from every fee charged. Want to pay your uncle Joe 25 cents per transaction for helping you? We can do that. Want to pay up to 5 different people? Sure, no problem. Just let us know who to pay and how much, and we'll take care of all of that for you so you can concentrate on your business. Your account will be credited with the remaining residual commissions less any network fees after we pay everyone you tell us to.

Opportunities in the ATM Business

Is owning and operating ATMs the only option?

While owning and operating the ATM machines yourself will result in the largest passive income, if you don't have the funds to start off owning your own ATMs, there are many other ways to earn a passive income in the ATM Business.

Being an ATM Site Locator

There are several ATM business options that don't require a capital investment (buying machines or loading cash). One of the opportunities is to become an ATM Site Locator.

An ATM site locator is a person who finds the locations that are interested in having an ATM in or at their location. This can be a retail store, a commercial building, a manufacturing facility, a strip mall, parking lot, or even bank branding opportunities, etc.

You can be the person who finds out who the right person is to talk to and then negotiate terms as if it were your own machine. Then work with an ATM company to have another IAD put their ATM machine in that location. There are several other pieces to the equation like who is going to load the cash (could be you, the location, or another 3rd party, etc.).

Suffice it to say, however, the more the site locator does, the more he/she can earn. For example, if you found a good location, and the owner of the location also didn't want to make the capital investment in the hardware but was willing to load the cash, you could theoretically share the surcharge with the hardware owner and give a piece of that to the location for loading the cash.

There are many ways to make a deal work, and learning the lingo and what makes a win-win for everyone is key to making the right deal. This is to just give you an example

The Amazing Money Machine

of how to enter the passive income ATM business without having to purchase your own ATM machines. Obviously, if you have the cash and found a good location, you would want to install your own machine to maximize the revenue, but if you wanted to start slow, just leverage existing relationships to get a lot of locations quickly, do not have $25,000 sitting around for 10 locations, or just need help from an ISO or IAD, you can leverage the relationship so you can get some passive income going. Eventually, you will have the funds to add more machines to your own portfolio.

Selling the ATM and Service to the Location

Sometimes, the owner of a location does not want someone to put an ATM into their place of business or other type of location. They may prefer to operate the ATM themselves and reap the rewards as well.

In this case, you can sell them the ATM hardware (with a small mark-up for a commission) and keep some or all of the interchange as your passive income. While it's not nearly as lucrative as getting the surcharge, your risk is completely removed. It goes back to the old adage: The

192

higher the risk, the higher the reward. While owning an ATM and loading it is not very risky, it is obviously a lot less risky to not do anything and still earn a small passive income.

What if I just want to be the Cash Loader (Vaulter)

This is another easy way to get into this ATM business. If you don't have locations, but live in an area when you see many ATMs, you can offer your cash loading service to the locations (especially if you see "out of order" signs often).

You can also contact ATM companies and tell them that you are a private ATM vaulter. You can come up with a schedule of fees based on distance to the location. Sometimes, a vaulter can make up to $0.50 or $0.75 per transaction or more, depending on how busy the location is and how much cash the ATM goes through.

ATM Depot often seeks out vaulters when off-site deployers prefer not to pay for armored car service for locations where that service can't be justified based on the added expense.

Want to know more about other ways to operate your ATM business? Check out the ATM Depot members' area.

Conclusion

With this, we come to the end of our book on setting up an ATM business. By now, you should have a clear idea of what is required for you to set up your own ATM business.

When you go through the book in order, you will find it covers the pertinent information you need to understand the ATM business. Now, it's up to you to put what you have learned into action.

Here's a recap:

The basics of an ATM business, including what it is and how it works

How to choose a location for placing an ATM

How do you make money?

Your role and responsibility

Who installs and programs the machines?

Who loads and reloads the machines?

Which machines are the best?

How do you arrange the cash to load into the machines?

Learning to operate the machine

The different revenue streams you can set up

Security features you can add to your ATM locations

Optional hardware for your machines

We have tried to be as detailed as possible, given that the average person doesn't know much about ATM machines or ATM businesses. This is why each chapter is quite comprehensive in scope and includes anything even remotely relevant to running an ATM business, as well as a little bit of redundancy on important aspects. Our aim is to not only educate you about establishing an ATM business, but to make it successful.

It is surprising to see that ATM machines are an everyday item, yet not many people actually think of making a living through them. After reading this book, you can.

The only requirement for you is to follow the tips and procedures provided. If you do so, you should have no problem setting up an ATM business and making it successful.

I wish you all of the success in the world, and should you want to get your own business up and running or already have a location in mind, please visit ATMDepot.com or call us at 888-959-2269.

Appendix

Most of this information is available on ATMDepot.com or on our blog.

You can also get more information by subscribing to our YouTube Channels.

> https://www.youtube.com/user/atmprocessing
> https://www.youtube.com/user/atmdepot

As well as liking any of our facebook pages

> https://www.facebook.com/ATMDepot
> https://www.facebook.com/getanatm

If you plan to work with ATMDepot.com we welcome the chance to help you succeed.

How To Load Cash Video: You can find this on our YouTube Channel. However, we plan to add a lot of videos to our member area where we walk you through not only how to load cash, but the settlement process and other important functions you've read about.

How Your ATM Gets Delivered: A video showing how the ATM arrives, what to look for when it arrives, and what to check to ensure it has arrived in working order.

How To Resolve Common ATM Related Issues:

ATM Error Codes to common issues with typical resolutions can be found on our website.

Our exclusive Members Area is available to Independent ATM Deployers wanting to get access to specific information. This is an example of what our IADs can find in our Members Area.

Besides our 24/7 Technical support, our Standard and Pro Member Areas include:

How to and Help Videos on topics such as:

> What to Say to Store Owners
> How and where to Find Good ATM Locations
> How to Change the ATM Lock Combo
> What are Master Keys and Convelops
> And much more

How to and Helpful Audio files for listening on the go:

Step by Step Instructions on how to program a Hyosung Halo
Sales Scripts
Overcoming Objections
And much more

Document Samples:

Equipment Order Forms
Merchant Applications
ACH forms
Placement Agreement Samples
Site Location Agreement (SLA)

Sample Sales Scripts:

These scripts help you to understand how to approach the building or retail owners. It will also help you to understand what to say and how to handle objections and much more.

We are constantly updating the Members Area. New information is added, and old and outdated information is purged, keeping the Members Area up-to-date so you only get the information that matters. No hype, no fluff.

Noah C. Wieder

NOTES:

NOTES:

Made in the USA
Columbia, SC
27 September 2020